They Made a Difference:
Memories of Mennonite Workers in Puerto Rico

Rafael Falcón, Tom Lehman
Editors

2021

Colección Menohispana

1. Puerto Rico: Island of Progress

2. La Obra Menonita en Puerto Rico, 1943-1981

3. Mennonite Memories of Puerto Rico

4. Memorias Menonitas de Puerto Rico

5. Historia del Menonitismo Hispanohablante: 1917-1990

6. Growing Up Mennonite in Puerto Rico: Nuestras Memorias

7. Hurricane María: Stories of Resilience and Compassion

8. They Made a Difference: Memories of Mennonite Workers in Puerto Rico

Titles in the *Colección Menohispana* series are available at Amazon.com. Profits from sales of these books are donated to Academia Menonita Betania.

Cover photo by R.J. Hower shows men from the Mennonite Service Organization, predecessor of Mennonite Disaster Service, rebuilding the clinic at Rabanal after Hurricane Betsy / Santa Clara destroyed it in 1956..

ISBN: 9798738552595

CONTENTS

DEDICATION

To those who came to the Island from the Continent and inspired a convincingly energetic faith, you were successful.

To those *boricuas* who joined these newcomers, partnered with them, and adapted that faith to the existing culture, you were successful.

ACKNOWLEDGMENTS

We want to thank Galen Greaser and Christine Falcón for their much appreciated contribution to the editing process. We were fortunate that at the last minute Bryan Falcón provided his help enhancing the photos in the book, noticeably improving it. Also we would like to give warm recognition to Rolando Santiago for all his support and words of encouragement.

In addition, we want to thank all the writers for their willingness to share memories of many of those who made a difference in the Mennonite work in Puerto Rico. Without their recollections, this book would not have been possible.

Rafael Falcón
Tom Lehman

PREFACE

Why another book on the Mennonite experience in Puerto Rico? After all we have already published seven books in the Colección Menohispana, including Justus Holsinger's 1982 book on the Mennonite church in Puerto Rico, *Mennonite Memories of Puerto Rico*, and *Growing up Mennonite in Puerto Rico*. Clearly we are suffering from some kind of fixation on the *Isla del Encanto* and the experiences of Mennonites on it!

We both grew up in the Mennonite milieu in Puerto Rico. That experience impacted and formed us. For us it was a wonderful experience, a safe, caring environment. In one way or another, we have tried to keep alive and share that experience, through books, photos, celebrations.

As many of the pioneers of the Mennonite work in Puerto Rico have begun to pass on to their reward, it seemed like a good time to gather memories of them, to help remember and honor those whose work made it all possible.

We originally toyed with title *Pillars of the Mennonite Work in Puerto Rico* for this book. Almost immediately that began to seem problematic. Who was or was not a pillar? We did not feel qualified to judge. By the accident of where and when we lived in Puerto Rico we knew some people better than others. The title *They Made a Difference* that we chose instead seemed to us to put the emphasis where it should be—on the work that was accomplished and on the group effort that made it possible. All who participated in it helped made a difference.

We started by sending out a call for memories of people who were involved in the Mennonite work in Puerto Rico. We were gratified by the response. As you will see, the memories are highly variable: some are long, some short, some recount personal interactions while others offer a summary of the person's life and involvement in the Mennonite work in Puerto Rico.

One thing we were glad to see was the good number of memories and recognition of the role of women in the Mennonite work in Puerto Rico. In the article "'Finding my place as a lady missionary:' Mennonite Women Missionaries to Puerto Rico, 1945-1960," written by Beth E. Graybill and published in *Journal of Mennonite Studies, vol. 17, 1999*, the author states that women were instrumental in building the Mennonite Church in Puerto Rico. They outnumbered male missionaries by almost two to one. All who were part of that milieu can testify to the many contributions of women to the Mennonite work in Puerto Rico and to the difference they made.

Inevitably, we were not able to identify or obtain memories of all who served in Puerto Rico and deserve to be recognized. We hope that the ones we have been able to include will capture the selfless spirit of service and caring that animated almost all who participated in this endeavor.

Tom Lehman

1

JUAN COLÓN

Don Juan Colón was one the first *boricuas* to become a member of the Puerto Rican Mennonite Church, and continued to be very active until his death. With the denomination being a new presence on the Island, Don Juan joined its efforts as a church planter and helped it to grow through his personal witness. He was a member on several boards as the Mennonite work developed, including involvement on the Academia Menonita Betania board of directors. Don Juan Colón was a successful landowner and farmer in the *barrio* of La Plata.

J uan Colón was born on January 27, 1915 and died on February 8, 1999. He was born in Aibonito and died in Cape Coral, Florida. He was married to María Celina Ortiz. They had seven children and an adopted daughter: Juan, Héctor, Benjamín, Wilfredo, Lilliam, Margarita, Samuel and Josefina (adopted).

When he began to interact with the Mennonite work he lived in the *barrio* Rabanal de Cidra neighborhood and planted tobacco to support his family. After he converted to the Lord he understood that he should no longer plant tobacco. The Mennonite mission gave him work on the La Plata farm, and in 1956 we moved to the La Plata neighborhood of Aibonito, to a house that belonged to the Mennonite mission and was located on one of their farms. Later they sold him the house along with the farm and he dedicated himself to raising chickens for To-Ricos and working in the Mennonite work until his retirement.

When my dad gave himself to the Lord he left everything he understood from the Bible that God did not like. He taught us to love the Lord and learn from his Word by having family worship every night. He and my mother began to work tirelessly for the Lord. They did a lot of personal work visiting the church families and going wherever they were needed two or three times a week.

He worked with Melquiades Santiago in the work of Rabanal de Cidra. Together with José A. Santiago they began the work at Honduras de Cidra. He was a pastor at the Guavate church and during that time the church reached the highest attendance numbers it has ever had. He served on the Mennonite Hospital board for 37 years as a representative of the Mennonite Church.

In his retirement years, already ill, he worshipped for a time at Summit Hills Church while living in Río Piedras. Then he returned to La Plata and attended the Church of Honduras. He later attended the church in La Plata until his wife died. After my mother died he came to live with me, Lilliam, in Cape Coral Florida, where he died.

He was a man completely given over to the Lord's work, an authentic servant of God, passionate about Jesus. The best legacy he left us was knowing the Lord and setting an example for us with his personal life. Today a grandson, Carlos Juan Colón, with his wife Emma, and a granddaughter, Linet Colón, with her husband José Luis, pastor two Mennonite churches.

What a blessing that the Mennonites came to Puerto Rico. I will be grateful to the Lord all my life for them.

Lilliam Colón González

2

JOHN DRIVER

John was born and raised in Hesston, Kansas. Prior to his assignment in Puerto Rico he had served in Civilian Public Service in a Bureau of Reclamation Project in Hill City, South Dakota, and in State Mental Health Hospitals in Howard, Rhode Island (just outside of Providence), and Poughkeepsie, New York. Bonny, his wife, came from Jackson, Minnesota, and was a graduate of the La Junta Mennonite School of Nursing.

He served in the La Plata Service Unit, first as a cook in the hospital and then as a medical social worker, from November 1945 to July 1948. Bonny served in the hospital as operating room supervisor from January 1947 to July 1948.

They returned to Puerto Rico in August 1951 under the auspices of Mennonite Board of Missions. They served in a pastorate in La Plata, Aibonito, until 1954, then in Palo Hincado, Barranquitas, until 1956. They lived in La Plata and John taught in the recently organized Bible Institute and at the same time pastored the congregation in Barrio Guavate, Cayey, until 1959, when the family moved to the Metropolitan Area to pastor an emerging congregation in the city. In about 1964 they moved to the town of Aibonito, where John served as pastor until 1966.

In January, 1967, the Drivers moved to Montevideo, Uruguay, where John served as Academic Dean and Professor of Church History and New Testament in the Inter-Mennonite Seminary until it was closed in 1974. In 1975 they were assigned to service in Spain, where over a period of nearly ten years they served in church planting and theological education. During this time they returned to Buenos Aires, Argentina, for a one-year assignment in theological education. In 1985 they took an assignment at the Mennonite Study and Retreat Center in Montevideo, Uruguay, where John taught and worked on manuscripts for publication. Prior to their retirement in July, 1989, the Drivers spent six months in Santa Cruz, Bolivia, where John was invited to teach in the Evangelical University in that city.

In retirement John has continued to receive invitations to offer seminars in seminary and church contexts throughout Latin America, both under the auspices of SEMILLA, with headquarters in Guatemala, and of national conferences and theological institutions.

———◦———

M any pastors spend much of their time in their dungeons or offices preparing sermons that in a matter of time will become obsolete and forgotten.

This story is a sermon in action about a deed of kindness. Deeds of kindness especially in times of need are never forgotten. One of the pastors of our small church in Coamo Arriba was "el hermano Driver," as my father liked to call him, who in turn called my father "hermano Mariano." These men were of two different colors and two different cultures, but had a unique sense of immense brotherhood.

Our little house was smack in the middle of a well-traveled path and an oasis for tired travelers. There was always fresh water, coffee, seasonal fruits and usually an admonition from my father who, without degrees, was a teacher, theologian, and lawyer of the community.

Every Wednesday and Sunday afternoon John Driver made the long and lonely journey from Palo Hincado to Coamo Arriba on horseback. He always stopped to chat with my father, and we children eagerly awaited his visit, as he seldom came empty handed. We always looked for the little brown paper sack full of candy and sometimes overripe bananas or plantains. But, oh, how we loved the candy, since we didn't have money or access to different kinds of sweets, which was very special for us children. So, we seldom remember the sermons, but deeds of kindness are never forgotten.

I shared this story with my Sunday school class at the church we attend in Ohio. The following Sunday our pastor, who is a hunter, brought me a package of frozen deer meat from his freezer.

Currently we winter in Coamo Arriba and our house is smack in the middle of the old *camino* that John Driver traveled. Many nights I think of him, wondering how in the world he traveled on those dark and dangerous roads on horseback.

The God of Moses and Abraham had to be watching over him.

Elena Ortiz Hershberger

A person who helped us as a family was John Driver. He introduced me to pastoral work in Summit Hills and in 1962 he officiated at my wedding with Lora Esch at the Summit Hills Church. Then, in 1970, he was instrumental in securing a grant from Mennonite Board of Missions so that we could go to the Mennonite Seminary in Montevideo, Uruguay, to study for two years. And here at Greencroft in Goshen, Indiana, he was present at our 50th wedding anniversary and helped us to renew our wedding vows.

Ángel Luis Miranda

3

CAROL GLICK KAUFMAN

Carol Glick Kaufman was from Sugarcreek, Ohio. She served with Civilian Public Service (CPS) in Ypsilanti, Michigan, before volunteering in Puerto Rico. She served in the La Plata Mennonite Project from 1944 to 1945. On the Island she was involved mainly in education, teaching at the Academia Bautista de Barranquitas and at the Escuela Menonita Betania in Pulguillas, where she was the director for many years. She was instrumental in helping Betania grow and become what it is today. In fact, whenever Mennonite education in Puerto Rico is mentioned Carol Glick Kaufman's name is at the fore. She died in 2008, when she was 86 years old.

C arol was my aunt, the sister of my father Leon, and always "Aunt Carol" to us, since I also have a sister named Carol.

Carol graduated from Goshen College in the early 1940s and went to Puerto Rico, where she stayed most of her life. Our family knew her from visits to her home area of Holmes County, Ohio. She also studied again at Goshen College for a semester or year in the early 1960s while I was a student at the college. I also visited her in Sarasota, Florida, when she was teaching there.

When she came to visit us in Ohio while I was growing up, I remember Carol as always happy and enthusiastic about everything, but especially about Puerto Rico and about serving the Lord. She would play ball with us and surprise us when she couldn't remember a word in English, only in Spanish. Aunt Carol was always one of my favorite relatives and I wanted to visit her in Puerto Rico. That happened twice while I was working for Goshen College and Mennonite Central Committee (MCC). The first time I was visiting Study Service Term units in Central America and Haiti and made a stop to see Carol. We had a wonderful time. She showed me around all her favorite places on the island. The second time our family of six stopped to see Aunt Carol on our way back from Bolivia, where we spent four years working with MCC. Aunt Carol bought a bakery birthday cake for our daughter Kimberly's first birthday. We all remember that— probably the only birthday cake any of us ever had from a bakery.

After moving to Arcadia, Florida, when she finally retired, Carol married my father's best friend, Paul Kaufman. We spent time with them in Florida and they visited us in Ohio. Carol had some wonderful years with Paul before Alzheimer's brought her life to a close. Aunt Carol was a special part of the Glick family, and we were all profoundly impressed with how she chose to spend her life.

Bruce Glick

I feel honored to share a few words about a person who followed her sense of call to serve God among the people in Puerto Rico.

As a young person growing up in the Mennonite Church in Puerto Rico, I knew who Carol Glick was before I knew her as a friend. I believe that most people in the Mennonite Church in Puerto Rico knew of Carol Glick. She was a faithful attendee of conference events, always reminding people of the importance of Christian education.

Like many others before me who sought her counsel, I remember a particular evening when I drove up and down the curvy roads of Pulguillas and then up that steep drive to visit with Carol at her home and seek her wisdom. I was being asked to become the school administrator at Academia Menonita in Summit Hills, and I did not know what to do. She encouraged me to step forth, assured me of her support, and reminded me of the importance of trusting in God, regardless of the circumstances. I left Carol's house that evening with a sense of knowing what God was calling me to do and a sense of security because of her willingness to walk with me.

Carol had the heart of a teacher. She used every opportunity— big or small—as a teachable moment. Her loving heart always put others before herself. I am quite aware of the personal sacrifices she made on many occasions to help and assist others.

Her faith was deeply rooted in the Anabaptist theological framework of how to understand scriptures and see the world. However, her faith was not just one of intellect and heart, but also a faith that was put into practice on a daily basis. As a young, inexperienced and, at times, very impatient administrator, I would walk into her office at the end of a long day to complain about this or that person. She would always listen. If she didn't have the time, she made time. Also, at the end of these conversations, which soon became part of my routine, I would see her smile and I knew what she was going to say, "Carlos, you might not need to like everybody; you just simply have to love them." In those few seconds—with the loving heart of a mother and with the strength and wisdom of a church leader—she had taught me once again!

Carol was a faithful person. Her faith in God never wavered. Even in the midst of difficulties she would remind others of the need to keep their eyes looking to God. When faced with financial challenges at the school and pushes for "more development work," her response was simple: "Let us take time to pray." Moreover, the results were indeed amazing. Year after year enough money came in to pay the bills. One way or another, God always provided!

I also had the opportunity to serve with her for several years on the executive committee of the Puerto Rico Mennonite Conference. We spent hours in the car driving back and forth from San Juan to Aibonito. I do have to admit that after several times of simply alternating drivers, she volunteered to drive all the time! As she used to tell me, "You are a city boy."

Carol took her call seriously. After living for years up in the mountains in the Aibonito area, she did what nobody ever thought she would do—moved to San Juan. In fact, she shared with me that she told God once in a prayer that God would have to pull her by her hair all the way from Aibonito to San Juan if she was meant to move. She often reminded me of this when she would hear me use the word "never." She would say to me, "Never use never as a response to God's call." When searching for guidance in my own life, she would remind me that Christians should not be surprised by what God might call them to do. Well, I have been surprised—actually quite surprised—by where God has called me. But she taught me well with her words, "When God calls, you simply follow."

There are so many stories, funny and serious, I could tell. Like the time Carol invited Celina and me to eat at a restaurant she had always wanted to visit but never had. After the wonderful meal, when it was time to pay the bill she realized she had forgotten to bring money! We all had a good laugh. Or the time that a late Friday evening conversation spent "dreaming about the future" led to Monday morning, with both of us in a plane traveling to Ohio to meet with a potential donor. Or the time when we, as conference leaders, needed to confront a particular situation and walked into the room not sure what we were going to say but with the assurance that God was in our midst.

Carol's work and ministry have touched and affected many people. You cannot visit Academia Betania without seeing the results of her hard work; hear about the strong academic reputation of Academia Menonita in Summit Hills without realizing that she laid the groundwork and the foundation for that; or meet women leaders in the conference today without discovering the important role she played as a teacher, role-model, and mentor. During our years in the executive committee she helped make the decision to license the first women for ministry. Ultimately, it is not what she did, but the people she touched that provide the real story of why Carol was such an influential person. The real story is found in the hearts—many more than any of us can know—that she touched, in the people she helped, never expecting anything in return, and in the lives that were influenced by her and changed forever.

The seeds that she has planted over the years have given fruit. Some of the trees have produced fruit that has continued to multiply while others are still growing. Her work and ministry will continue because those of us who had the privilege of having Carol as part of our lives will always remember her and because many of us realize that where we are and who we are is because of her love, patience, and caring.

Carlos Romero

After my family began attending the Mennonite church during the decade of the 1950s, we frequently heard the name of Carol Glick mentioned, particularly in the area of Christian education. We overheard, too, something related to her work as director of the Escuela Menonita Betania that was rather unusual in our thinking for a woman to do during those years. It seemed that Carola, as she was known in Puerto Rican circles, had acquired a chauffeur's license in order to help pick up students to take them to the school and was driving one of the two trucks renovated with benches in the covered rear end of the vehicles.

My first direct contact with Carola, though, came in 1968 when she hired me to work at the Academia Menonita Betania. As a recent college graduate, she employed me to teach Spanish and social studies to the seventh, eighth and ninth grade students. I will always remember her wholehearted commitment and dedicated energy to the mission of the school as its years-long administrator. Even more impressive to me personally is the memory of her support of my work and ideas as a rookie teacher, and her wise and appropriate advice.

A stronger bond with Carola came in 1973, when she hired me as her assistant director. After a few months she strongly urged me to become the school's director. Carola was ready for a break and had some ideas she wanted to explore. To put it mildly, I was not only surprised with the suggestion but rather intimidated by it. At the time I was only 25 years old, and I would be the first Puerto Rican director. In its twenty-six years of existence, it had operated under the leadership of United States-born administrators. Yet, she believed in me, trusted me, and mentored me, offering me her support and advice. Through this, Carola put action into a belief she thought was right, passing the torch onto Island-based leadership.

Close to twenty years later, in 1989, our family decided to spend my first sabbatical from Goshen College on the Island of Enchantment, and we needed a place to live for a year. We searched for a house in Aibonito, but nothing seemed to materialize. Then one day my father mentioned our situation to Carola. What a relief when he shared the option she gave him of renting her home in Pulguillas for a very reasonable price! Needless to say, we very much enjoyed that year of living in her home, with its scenery of mountains, distant towns, and the Caribbean.

During that year our younger son became a direct recipient of Carola's benevolent spirit. As a fifth-grader adjusting to a new home and classes in Spanish, he made friends with Naipi, a stray dog attempting to live on the school grounds. With new residents living in the houses on campus and no one apparently taking care of the little black-and-white fellow, Brent wanted to bring him home to our place. Our son was suggesting we could transport the dog to our house by car, but I was very reluctant to drive him home with his dirty fur and all his fleas. Frankly, I was not very excited about the idea of adoption, but hauling him in my clean car really bothered me. Carola, though, who was listening to our conversation, came to the rescue. She offered to take the puppy to our house, along with his dish, and even a little dog house for him, and managed to convince me that Naipi could be an excellent companion for Brent. She was right. The dog lived with us, endeared himself to our family, and made that year a special one for us all. Carola, meanwhile, has left memories in our hearts of what she was, a very special human being.

Rafael Falcón

4

MIRIAM GODSHALL

Mim was born on March 11, 1937, in Harleysville, Pennsylvania. After becoming a nurse she volunteered for two years of service with the Mennonite Board of Missions and was assigned to the Aibonito Mennonite Hospital, where she served from 1960 to 2017. In 1975 she studied midwifery in San Juan and became one of a few certified midwives on the island. She delivered over 4,500 babies during her years in Puerto Rico. She has been recognized in Puerto Rico with several awards for her contributions. She now lives in Harrisonburg, Virginia.

M iriam Godshall was born on March 11, 1937, at her parent's farm home in Harleysville, Pennsylvania, the firstborn of Paul and Stella Godshall. She developed rheumatic fever around age 11 and spent six months resting on the sofa in our home. Her primary goal in life was to become a nurse. When she first made application to the nursing program at Grandview Hospital, Sellersville, Pennsylvania, she was rejected because of a heart murmur, which had developed as a result of her rheumatic fever illness years before. However, an internist intervened and cleared her for studies.

She earned her RN degree and then decided to volunteer for two years of voluntary service under the Mennonite Board of Missions. They accepted her application and assigned her to work at Hospital Menonita in Aibonito, Puerto Rico in 1960. After her two years of service she decided to stay on as a paid nurse at the hospital.

She developed a love and skill for delivering babies and in 1975 studied midwifery in San Juan, Puerto Rico, becoming one of a few certified mid-wives on the island. She continued living in Aibonito, providing a lifetime of service at the hospital. She delivered 4,645 babies.

She participated in the Aibonito Mennonite Church as a Sunday school teacher, as a church pianist and choir participant, and as a secretary creating the Sunday church bulletins.

Her 57 years of life and service in Aibonito was honored on several occasions. In 2009 she was featured in an article about midwifery in Puerto Rico in the *San Juan Star*. In 2014 she received an award from the Council of Midwifery of Puerto Rico honoring her work. On April 18, 2016 a classroom in the Preparatory High School in Aibonito was named and dedicated to Mim, honoring her as a model for servanthood. On that occasion she received the keys to the town of Aibonito from Mayor William Alicea Pérez. She was celebrated again in an all-day Sunday event at the Aibonito Mennonite Church on August 6,

2017, as she was saying her farewells. She remained in her house until its sale was confirmed, and then suffered through Hurricane María on September 18, 2017 before leaving the island and coming to Harrisonburg, Virginia on October 10, 2017.

She now resides at Park Place in Virginia Mennonite Retirement Community in Harrisonburg.

Stan Godshall

M im served in Puerto Rico from 1960 to 2017.
Mim and I were housemates from 1965 to January 2001. Mim was a very dedicated nurse working nights most of the time until she took a midwifery course. I'm not sure of the year but I think it was 1965 or 1966. Her life changed a bit to giving prenatal classes and doing deliveries. This was her life's joy. She loved her work helping to prepare ladies for this wonderful event of new life and to include the husband and father-to-be in the experience. She has quite a few stories to tell from the 4,645 deliveries she has done, besides helping with many more. Hospital Menonita and Miss Godshall were quite widely known. There was a couple living on a boat off the coast of Puerto Rico that came for classes and did some calculating to know how to come to the hospital in time, when it was time! Mim and I received an invitation to their boat sometime after the delivery. It was an interesting experience to visit them. Mim has other stories she has written down of patients' gratitude for her services. She did one home delivery, but you will need to contact her for the details.

Besides nursing, Mim loved to work with children in the church and she used her omnichord to sing with them. Montessori School was another place she went with regularity to sing with the children and her omnichord. She has stories from there also. A lawyer was visiting the class one day and telling of his memories of Mim coming and singing with them in Montessori, when who should appear but Mim.

Mim and her omnichord also went to cheer older people as well and to hospital singing on Tuesday evenings.

Mim prepared the church bulletin for many years and was

always ready to offer a helping hand in whatever church activity there might be.

Serving the Lord through the hospital and church was Mim's life.

She was and is a good friend and encourager.

Wanda Brunk Zimmerly

To Mim Godshall, my sister in the faith of Our Lord Jesus Christ.

What a joy it is to know you and to think back on our times together.

As I go down memory's lane, I remember:
- Meeting in 1963
- Sharing in the routine of life as we worked and lived together
- Sharing a house and tasks
- My driving and you not wanting to
- You doing more of the cooking
- Going to hospital singing
- Participating in the Youth Group
- Teaching Sunday school
- Traveling together to Africa, Switzerland, Haiti, World Conference in Brazil, and Florida.

Also I think of your special abilities:
- Attending more than 4,598 deliveries and assisting many more
- Giving "Prepared Childbirth" classes
- Playing your omnichord to spread love to people of all ages
- Your enthusiasm for raising a garden and flowers
- Doing the church bulletin for many years
- I appreciate you for who you are and what you have added to my life, your enthusiasm and encouragement.

I wish you God's richest blessings as you begin another era of your life seeking God's direction in how you are to serve Him as you have in the past and as you face the challenges of change.

My love and prayers go with you,

Wanda Brunk Zimmerly
July 24, 2017

5

ANNABELLE GREASER

Annabelle Troyer Greaser, daughter of George and Kathryn (Sommers) Troyer, was born in Chicago in 1921 and grew up in India. In 1944 she graduated from La Junta (Colorado) Mennonite School of Nursing. The Mennonite Board of Missions assigned her to work at the hospital in La Plata, Puerto Rico. There she met and married Lawrence H. Greaser in 1946. She and her husband were missionaries to Puerto Rico from 1950 to 1971.

She devoted much of her time to her husband and five children, but also found ways to serve in the church. She liked to write, and several of her articles, including one on the joys of motherhood, appeared in Mennonite publications. Annabelle died in 1974 at the early age of 52.

———◦———

A nnabelle Greaser, daughter of George and Kathryn Troyer, grew up in India. As a young adult she focused on an education that would be useful as a missionary to India. She was one of the first women to study theology at Goshen College and then completed her nursing degree. When she went to the Mennonite Board of Missions to apply as a missionary to India, it was the middle of World War II and they were not eager to send a single woman there during the war. Instead, they suggested that she join her parents, who were then in Puerto Rico. She did this and worked at the hospital in La Plata.

A few months after arriving, she and a friend went to San Juan to pick up Lawrence Greaser and R.J. Hower. Her friendship with Lawrence grew and before long they were engaged and married. After Civilian Public Service ended, they moved to Kansas so Lawrence could finish his degree. Within two years they had three children, Galen, David and Daniel, who kept them on their toes. Dr. Troyer invited them to return to Puerto Rico in 1950 to work on an agriculture project in Pulguillas. Later on Joe and Rachel joined the family.

Lawrence worked long hours, especially when he was pastoring the Betania church during Lester Hershey's furlough. Part of the ministry included riding a horse down the mountain to visit a church in Coamo Arriba. One night a big rainstorm came up and he waited it out in the church. Annabelle was home, wondering if he had fallen off the mountain or what had happened to him, as there was no way to communicate. It was not an easy task to do the main work of parenting their four young boys during those very busy years.

A large part of Annabelle's ministry was to her family, but she also found ways to serve in the church teaching Sunday school, doing visitation, working with the women's group and organizing summer Bible schools. Much of what she did was behind the scenes, not in the limelight. But if these women, Kathryn and

Annabelle, had not provided their support to George and Lawrence, the more visible ministries would not have been as effective. They directly impacted the work by their integrity, deeply held convictions, love for others, prayers and strong faith.

Lawrence and Annabelle both served Christ in Puerto Rico in the areas of church ministry, economic development, and hospital administration. In 1971 the decision was made that Puerto Rican pastors should lead the church. The Greasers moved to Goshen, Indiana and one year later Annabelle was diagnosed with cancer. She passed away after two years at the age of 52, much too early, but leaving a legacy that lives on in the lives she touched.

Rachel Greaser Good

6

LAWRENCE H. GREASER

Lawrence H. Greaser was born on February 17, 1922, near Garden City, Missouri, to the Charles and Pearl (Hershberger) Greaser family. As a conscientious objector, Lawrence served at the Terry, Montana, Civilian Public Service (CPS) camp and at Ypsilanti State Hospital in Michigan.

In 1945 he was transferred to the CPS unit in La Plata, Puerto Rico. In 1946 he married Annabelle Troyer in La Plata. The couple returned to Puerto Rico with their family in 1950. Over the next two decades Lawrence served as pastor of four congregations (Betania, Coamo Arriba, Usabón, Aibonito), was director of the Ulrich Foundation project and became the administrator of the Mennonite General Hospital in Aibonito.

Lawrence and his family moved to Goshen, Indiana, in 1971, where he administered the High Park Physicians group. From 1974 to 1986 Lawrence was the director for Latin America at the Mennonite Board of Missions. Lawrence died in 2015.

———◦———

T he son of a preacher man hears lots of preaching. Dad preached Sunday morning—and sometimes Sunday evening. Lester Hershey preached on the radio, and we listened. Billy Graham came to preach, and we went. Visiting preachers took the pulpit, and we lent an ear. And at church conferences everybody preached. Even Dr. Troyer—Grandpa to us— occasionally preached! The half-life of a sermon was, as a rule, even more fleeting than the short span of the information we crammed into our brains the night before an exam; and the end-life was reached soon after, well before next Sunday's sermon.

The words Dad preached have flowed down the river, along with most of what I've read, the lectures I sat through, and the movies I've watched, but I do recall at least the subject of some of his sermons, and sometimes a seed did fall on marginally fertile soil. The parable of the talents was the subject one Sunday morning. This parable can be interpreted in several ways, the most obvious being the idea that it exhorts us to use our God-given abilities in His service. On this subject, if I may say so, Dad practiced what he preached. He may not have been blessed with talents superior to those of most people, but he did have the impulse to make the most of what he was given.

What he was *not* given at an early age were the advantages of comfort or privilege. The 1920s and '30s in Missouri were hard times for many, including the Charlie Greaser family. Dad was born in a small house without electricity or indoor plumbing. Couch potatoes were unheard of in that family. Funny bones were okay; lazy bones were not. The work ethic was either inherited or acquired by the time the children were old enough to turn the eggs in the basement incubator or feed the pigs or haul the firewood. Charlie and Pearl Greaser's children were expected to be good and good for something. At age thirteen Dad got a head start on being good for something when he hired out to the neighboring farmer to do a grown man's job for the dollar a day wages the family needed. Had his life followed a simple script he might have become a good for something Missouri farmer, but it didn't.

In 1939 the family took the decisive, life-changing decision to uproot and move to Hesston, Kansas, so Dad and his siblings could continue their education. Eighth grade was as far as Dad had advanced. He began high school when most young people his age were graduating. After six weeks of the hot Kansas wind and English grammar he was ready to go back to Missouri and farm, but he stayed the course, finishing high school and one semester in Hesston College. With World War II still raging, the National Selective Service drafted him in June, 1943, one year before the Allied's D-Day invasion of Normandy.

After being subjected to the verbal abuse and threats that officers and enlisted men dispensed to conscientious objector during the physical exam at Fort Leavenworth, Kansas, he was sent to a Civilian Public Service (CPS) Camp in Terry, Montana. At Camp Terry he was assigned to the kitchen, peeling potatoes for 150 men, serving tables and washing dishes. Then, in December, 1943 he agreed to a transfer to Ypsilanti State Hospital in Michigan, where he worked the night shift for fourteen months as a patient attendant in the men's violent ward of this psychiatric hospital, before taking the day shift for another eleven months. The emotional toll of the experience lingered even after he was unexpectedly asked to report to Mennonite Central Committee for transfer to a CPS unit in Puerto Rico.

Over time Dad acquire skills that allowed him to serve in many ways. Many of these skills he acquired on-the-job, by answering the call to fill positions he may not have initially felt adequately prepared for. His repertoire of skills is testament to his positive and optimistic nature and his courage to accept new challenges, confident that God would help him find a way to do them well.

23

He could preach the sermon and sing the solo, weld a pipe and write the budget, run a bulldozer and design a building, raise a family and manage a hospital, grow cucumbers and supervise the mission program in Latin America for the Mennonite Board of Missions. He could serve up a great waffle breakfast and then help wash the dishes.

A story told by Ana Beatriz Torres Hernández in her book *Sistema de Salud Menonita: Una Página Extraordinaria de la Historia de Puerto Rico*, illustrates the point. A visitor in tie and suit came to the hospital in Aibonito asking to speak to the administrator. He was informed that Mr. Greaser was not in his office but could be found attending to a break in a four-inch water line that ran through the hospital. The visitor made his way to the location and asked for the administrator. To his amazement, his attention was directed to the trench where don Lorenzo stood hunched in mud-splattered overalls, welding torch in hand, repairing the break that had flooded the area.

During his time in Puerto Rico, which he considered a blessing and a privilege, Dad served in almost every area of the Mennonite presence there. At various times he was the mechanic, chaplain and administrator of the hospital; pastor of congregations at Betania, Coamo Arriba, Usabón and Aibonito; manager of a small private farm and later director of the much larger Ulrich Foundation experimental farm; and a mainstay of the Luz y Verdad choirs. The school of adversity and the example of nurturing parents helped form his character and taught him at an early age the value of helping, sacrificing, persevering, serving others and being grateful. The tough times molded a builder, leader, and doer, and in all things he was guided by a simple motto: "Follow the path of Jesus." In later years he looked back on his life with surprise and gratitude. In his words, "I am amazed and humbled at the way the Lord has blessed my life. The way the Lord has put his hand on that 'hired hand' in Missouri who didn't know what he wanted or should do and given me the opportunities of involvement in Kingdom work the way He has is nearly incomprehensible for me."

Dad grew up steeped in the fundamentalist religious views and political conservatism of rural mid-America. With age this could easily have hardened into the dogmatism, America first-ism, xenophobia, nativism, intolerance and bigotry shamefully often found today in evangelical circles. Among the things I most admired about Dad is that with age, while remaining steadfast in his faith, he grew in compassion, tolerance, willingness to change, and acceptance of the diversity of human experience. He retained the capacity to be surprised and amazed - "*cosa más grande, chico,*" he would often say, quoting comedian Tres Patines of *La Tremenda Corte*—and never lost his sense of curiosity and the eagerness to learn. He was born in the "show me" state and got his wish, having seen much of the world and enjoyed many of nature's wonders. He lived a full and active life, a compassionate, kind, and generous life, in the spirit of servanthood to which he felt called. Thanks for the example. In the Puerto Rico of yesteryears it was customary when leaving the presence of an elder to ask for his or her blessing as a demonstration of respect and appreciation. For old times' sake and when in need of reassurance I still hear myself saying at times "*Bendición, Papi.*" His ready reply soon follows, "*Que Dios les bendiga, hijo*".

Galen D. Greaser

One of the main things that stands out about my father's life is the way God led him. He often mentioned that he never went looking for jobs or positions, but they came to him. As a young man and conscientious objector to the war, Civilian Public Service gave him the jobs of cook, orderly at a psychiatric hospital and mechanic in La Plata. Dr. Troyer asked him to be a farm manager in Pulguillas and later the church in Betania needed his help. Ulrich Foundation came calling and asked him to be their farm administrator. The Aibonito Church was just being formed and was meeting at the Luz y Verdad buildings. The group asked Lawrence to be their pastor. This was a difficult decision for him but he felt God calling him, so how could he say no? While he was pastor in Aibonito, construction of the church began and he designed the two-stage building and was actively involved in the building process. The Mennonite Hospital asked him to be a chaplain and a few years later to be the administrator. Throughout his time in P.R. he also pastored small groups in Usabón and Coamo Arriba. As they were leaving Puerto Rico, High Park Physicians asked him to manage their group practice and while he was there Mennonite Board of Missions asked him to become the Director for Latin America, which he did until retirement.

As a P.K. (preacher's kid) I saw Lawrence spending hours on Saturdays preparing sermons, and Sundays preaching them, performing weddings and funerals, counseling people, helping grieving families, leading prayer meetings and business sessions, teaching, advising, loving his flock and bringing them closer to Christ.

Proverbs 18:16a says, "A man's gift makes room for him." Lawrence had many gifts. He was a man of integrity who loved God and others. He was always honest, trustworthy, and faithful to keep his promises. He was a leader, a planner and an administrator, always very organized and thinking ahead. He was a hard worker and made good use of his time. Lawrence was humble and was motivated by serving others, generously volunteering many hours in later years to his church and community. He did not want the glory for himself, but for God. He was conscientious about how he handled money, time and resources. Later in life he had time to explore his artistic side and worked with stone and wood to create beautiful pieces. He always loved music and singing and was asked to sing "Padre Nuestro" (Our Father) at many weddings. He enjoyed telling stories about the past. He was a good husband, father and grandfather and passed these qualities on to his family and others by his example and the way he lived.

Rachel Greaser Good

Shifting Truck Load (fragment from Lawrence Greaser autobiography)

At this time there was no Mennonite church in Aibonito although there were a number of members of the church living in Aibonito. I became a part of a group of persons who helped envision and facilitate the beginning of a new congregation in Aibonito. We began meeting in the recording studio of the Luz y Verdad building. The space was very inadequate for the group of approximately 60 to 70 attendees. At the request of the group and the Mission Board, in 1960 I resigned as administrator of the Foundation and became a full-time pastor of the new congregation in Aibonito.

I had been licensed for pastoral responsibilities at Betania and satellite congregations, Coamo and Coamo Arriba. When the Aibonito congregation was formed, I was asked to serve in a leadership role. The conference requested my ordination. I had been satisfied being an active "layperson" leader. Administration work at the Ulrich Foundation had been less stressful than the pastoral work in Betania, even though the experience at Betania and other congregations had been very positive. However, I could not but take seriously the call of the church for my ordination as the pastor of the new Aibonito congregation. After days and nights of "internal wrestling" I agreed to the request and on June 22, 1965, I was ordained for pastoral ministry. During our time at the church, 1960-1965, we built a large building in two stages. First we built the Sunday school annex which was used as an assembly hall until sufficient funds were available to build the sanctuary part. The second stage of the building process was completed in 1964.

The building process required the purchase of materials in San Juan. One day I borrowed the Ulrich Foundation truck and took off for San Juan with a big list of things needed, including 2x6 16-foot long lumber, long steel rods, etc. I knew that these materials were longer than the truck bed with the resulting physics consequences. Furthermore, by the time we had all of the materials on the truck it was higher (bigger) than what should normally be placed on a 1 1/2-ton truck. But this was no "normal" situation. This was "church work."

Highway #1 from San Juan to Ponce, on the south side of the island, goes through Aibonito. It was a two-lane road and included a section of the "famous" Caguas hill. This included steep, very tight curves. As trucks were going up the mountain they would "blow their horns" and stay on the left side of the road as they drove around the curves, and then get back on to the right side of the road. Oncoming traffic would stop until the trucks had made the "maneuver." I knew that I would need to follow this way of driving with my load.

Before leaving for the hills I chained the load down as best I could. The first part of the trip on the level roadway went very well. Before starting up the mountainous part of the road I stopped to see if all was well with the load. It was not!!! The load had shifted backward about 12 inches. Now what?? I dare not start up the mountain with that reality facing me. How could I get that load back in place on the truck? Fortunately or providentially, alongside of the highway a section of the road had been cut out when the highway was built, resulting in a vertical wall. Furthermore, there was enough room for me to back the truck toward that wall. After several bumps of the extended load against that wall the materials were all "back in place" on the truck bed. Next move? TIGHTEN the retaining chains as much as humanly possible and PRAY that the load of materials needed to build the Aibonito Mennonite church building would stay in place on that truck up over that mountain and around the multitude of curves ahead before reaching the destination of Aibonito. Thank God the load was in place as I drove in to the building site in Aibonito late that night. That was one of the longest trips I ever made between Aibonito and San Juan in the twenty years I lived there.

As I reflect on that experience these many years later it still scares me. What if that load of materials had fallen off onto the road?

From Lawrence Greaser's Autobiography

7

DAVID HELMUTH

David was born in Ohio on April 7, 1935. He served the church
in many capacities for over 40 years. As a youth he taught Bible
school and Sunday school in mission churches in Cleveland and
Congo, Ohio. He and his wife Naomi served in Puerto Rico
under the Mennonite Board of Missions from 1961 to 1973. His
roles there included teaching, pastoring and directing the
Mennonite Bible Institute. He passed away on September 26,
2020.

T o me, he was "Dad" or "Papi". To many others, he was "Pastor," "Pastor David," or "Reverendo Helmuth." Everywhere I went someone knew my father! How could this be the case? "Oh, you must be one of Dave and Naomi's boys." "Tu papá es David, no?" Where to begin an even reasonable attempt to write the numerous memories of my father.

My father was afflicted with vascular dementia in his final years. It was less than a month before his death that I received the invitation from the editors to contribute to this book of memories of the Mennonite "pillars" in Puerto Rico. Noting my father's name was on the list, I agreed to write something for this book, unlike other offers I had received for writings. I haven't considered myself a particularly good writer, but that assessment will be out of my hands. These selected memories of my dad are what has driven me to write this.

The Darkly Tanned American Pastor

Dad was nearly six feet tall, had big thick shoulders, arms, thighs and legs. He was a solid man of European descent who had become very strong in his early years with physical farm labor. This squareness allowed him to function as a well anchored position player on the family basketball *cancha*. He simply could not be budged, even by two or three of us boys at once. Dad also inherited coal black hair and skin which tanned merely by thinking about walking outside. It didn't take long in the Caribbean sun and the closer location to the equator for this Ohio boy to begin looking like a richly tanned *hombre latino*. Hats were not commonly worn by Midwesterners and I don't recall dad wearing one while in Puerto Rico. His face and neck became milk chocolate brown. Short sleeves were also the custom on the island for Dad. Thus, the back of his hands, forearms and lower upper arms became accustomed to the warmth and also darkened very quickly. Long pants were the norm of modest dress of the times.

For those who remember my mother, she was and is a typical Irish-English woman of paler complexion with strawberry blonde hair. My brothers and I all more closely resembled our mother in our younger years. To look at us boys   you would know who our mother was without a doubt. We had fine hair, blue eyes, light skin and were of slighter build, just like Mom. We were quite the contrast to our dark brown-skinned dad.

However, it didn't take very many trips to the *playa* on a Saturday to realize Dad really was just as pale as we boys. Once he took off his shirt and put on his plaid swimming trunks to go jump in the water with us, his exposed chest, shoulders and legs were just as milky white as ours! We were astonished at the contrast between his forearms and shoulders, for example. It was something which made us smile. After leaving the farm for college, seminary and Puerto Rico, he had finally obtained his "farmer's tan."

Sunday Evening Visiting Pastor and Ice Cream

Dad and Mom had five boys, Robin (me), Roy, Roger, Ray and Roland. My parent arrived in Puerto Rico with three of us in 1961. Two more were added in 1962 and 1965. With Dad working for the Mennonite Board of Missions, trying to learn Spanish well enough for public speaking, driving nowhere very quickly due to windy and narrow hillside roads, he was a very busy man. Mom kept us fed, clothed, mostly tamed and prevented us from seriously hurting each other. But time alone with only Dad was a relative rare commodity. It wasn't that we didn't like our siblings or needed to get away from home, it simply was special to be with Dad all by ourselves.

Occasions which allowed for one of us to be with Dad were when he would preach on Sunday evenings at a small community church, usually somewhere out in the hills of central Puerto Rico. I am not sure I could name all of the towns he visited. We had fun discussing among ourselves, prior to departure, whether Dad was going to preach a brand new sermon or whether he was going to deliver one of his previously used ones. After all, it was a different audience. They would not have known if it was new or refurbished.

Another fun part of these Sunday evening excursions and, perhaps, the real reason we wanted to go with Dad was ice cream. Dad grew up having ice cream on Saturday nights. For all I know, his parents and siblings may have had ice cream both Saturday and Sunday nights. But, on these visiting pastor occasions it was very common for Dad to stop for ice cream on the way back home. I am not sure if it was real ice cream or if it was flavored ice or ice milk or *paletas*. It didn't matter to me. It was good! Thanks to Dad, I have always loved ice cream as much as he did and as much as his parents did and his siblings still do.

Lined Up for Haircuts

For anyone who has lived on a missionary's salary, you will know money is relatively tight. Of course, having five children instead of one or two added to the expenses side of the budget equation. More on that later. Fortunately, Dad and Mom had all boys and no girls who may have required more attention to their hair. Dad might have been reluctant to use hair clippers on a daughter, but he was not afraid to use them on us Every month, although it seemed like every two weeks, we would get the word to begin filing past wherever Dad was stationed with the stool, towel, clothespin and clippers. I am not sure whether any scissors were involved in this process. All I remember is after each of our turns, we were to find Mom for her to inspect the results. If Dad had missed a spot or something was uneven, back we went for round two. Fortunately, I recall most haircuts were Saturday evenings, allowing us to shower and rinse off all of the scratchy trimmings. I am guessing these cuts were also scheduled so we would look nice(r) for church and because Saturday evenings were not optional bathing nights. But, they were not exactly evenings we looked forward to either.

Pastors Have Curfews for Their Kids, Too

Being a pastor's kid and a missionary's kid seemed to entail a lot of (probably, self-imposed) expectations. Even so, I recall being happy as a child and growing up quite worry free. I really had not spent much time outside of Puerto Rico my first 16 years of life because Mom and Dad moved to *la Isla del Encanto* when I was about four years old. That was the perfect age for me, as I wasn't old enough for school and could spend countless hours every day playing outside with neighborhood friends. This allowed me to learn Puerto Rican Spanish very quickly.

As I grew into my later elementary school years, middle school years and then into high school, many of the friends I went to church with also attended my school. Our Sunday morning classes were interesting, but our Sunday evening youth gatherings were simply fun. Since we lived within walking distance of home and town, it was not unusual for some of us to walk from church to downtown Aibonito after our Sunday evening church activities. Of course, I needed and always obtained permission to go. At least that is what I recall. With the permission came a curfew, which seemed perfectly reasonable to me. Since I was a tweener or early teenager, though, I once made the mistake of disregarding the curfew. I knew right away I was going to be late. I quietly came into our unlocked house and all was still. As I tiptoed from the living room toward the kitchen on the way to the back, Dad came quietly out of his bedroom and wanted to know why I was late. Without his customary glasses, he seemed upset and gruff. He wasn't. He didn't even want to know where I had been or what I had been doing. He simply wondered why I had disregarded the curfew. I apologized immediately, knowing I was in the wrong. There was no punishment that I recall, perhaps, because I didn't argue or because I admitted my mistake immediately. Oh, by the way, my friends and I were at the corner store gorging ourselves with pizza and soda pop!! We didn't have pop at home. Ever! And, the only pizza I recall having at home was from a Chef Boyardee boxed kit. You can't blame us for wanting pizza and pop. But, pastors and missionaries have curfews, too. I learned my lesson.

Too Many Kids! What Were You Thinking?

By now you know Dad and Mom had five boys. I was nearly five when my next to youngest brother was born and nearly eight and a half when the youngest was born. The two of them didn't cause me any problems. They slept in a bedroom with my middle brother, who was about three years younger than me. I slept in another bedroom with my next oldest brother. Actually, we slept in the same bed. This brother was also taller and stronger than I. He could run faster, could jump higher and was a better shot at basketball. He could also eat more. That was primarily, in my opinion anyway, because he had less self-control. So, he would help himself to more than his "share" of food at the table. Sometimes he would have his food on his plate before Dad would say, "Amen." Dad didn't seem bothered by this. But I also could not blame my brother for this. After all, he was hungry and growing fast, too. He was doing what came natural: getting some food! I was sure he might have been a more devout student of Dad's eating habits when we were young.

On an occasional Saturday night Mom would get us all bathed and into our pajamas while Dad would drive to the local Burger King. He would get four hamburgers, four small French fries and four small milk shakes. Three of those combinations would get split in half, with each of the five boys and Mom getting a half share. The fourth whole combination would go to Dad. At the time I didn't think anything about this system of allotment. Dad was bigger, he was an adult and he was a parent. What parents say is what goes.

Later in life, I found this system amusing and perplexing. Why not just get seven hamburgers, seven fries and seven shakes? Probably, because the youngest two brothers would not be able to eat a full combination anyway. More likely, though, was the expense of seven meals compared to four. There simply wasn't enough cash to spare for something which was considered a luxury by many.

When I had my own family, I came to understand the privileged position Dad had as well earned and well deserved. If he ate a whole hamburger, fries and shake and we only had half of each, that was okay. He worked to earn them. I should have been more grateful to Dad and Mom we even had Burger King once in a while.

However, being a normal self-absorbed, immature pre-teenager made it natural for me to criticize Dad one time about the size of our family. I remember sitting on a chair in our living room while

Dad was on the nearby couch. I laid into him about the numerous children (five), the fact we were so close together in age, and the fact I never even had a bed to myself. All of this meant we were needing lots of food to supply our stomachs and fuel our boundless energy. I came right out and scolded him for having "so many kids" and wondering if Mom and he "knew what they were doing." Dad was very calm and listened to me. He went about telling me how much they loved each one of us and how happy they were to have each one of us. It all made sense after we talked.

Many years later I asked Dad if he remembered this occasion. Fortunately, he said he had no recollection of this event. I even asked him on another occasion and he still had no recollection. I still apologized to him multiple times. I had come to realize the beauty of our parents being responsible for their family and our well-being. And they did a wonderful job. I hit the jackpot when it came to both my mom and my dad. I am grateful I had the opportunity to tell my mom and dad this on several occasions, especially, before Dad developed vascular dementia.

The Dad with Lots of Lessons for Me

As I mentioned, my dad was a wonderful father and my mom is a wonderful mother! I learned and am still learning from their lives and examples. Some of the life lessons I learned from my father include, in no particular order:

- Learn something every day. Dad and Mom ventured at a young age from rural Ohio across the sea to an island with a different culture, different language and lots of unknowns. Their twelve years there rewarded them with new customs, many friendships and expanded their view of the world. I have also strived to learn new angles, perspectives or ways of thinking.

- Have some fun every day. Whether it be wrestling three-on-one or exposing himself to the sun on the beach, Dad took time to have fun with us. I also strive to enjoy the outdoors, ride one of my bicycles, plan a hike or fun time with family and grandchildren.

\- Live within your means. Mom and Dad were very wise, deliberate and careful with the limited funds they were paid. They never complained. This lesson has served me well for many years and needs no additional explanation.

\- Apologize when you have wronged someone. Dad made it a point to apologize to Mom, neighbors or friends when he had offended them. I saw him do this on many occasions. I would say I am still learning this lesson, but I am better at it now compared to 40 years ago.

\- Make memories while you can. Dad prioritized participating in immediate as well as extended family gatherings. I think this may have been more important to him in his later years, both because Mom and he were abroad during much of their 20s and 30s (missing out on the extended gatherings then) and because Dad's late onset dementia clouded his memory bank of the gatherings of which he had been a part. This has also reminded me of the importance of making memories with my friends, my immediate family and others I cherish as I don't know what the day will bring.

\- Lastly, don't take yourself too seriously. By now you may have been thinking my dad was perfect. As I child, I thought he was. As a teenager, I sure did not think he was. As an independent adult, I know Dad realized he wasn't perfect. I also know he was not given to taking himself too seriously. His example of learning, enjoying life, living within one's means, apologizing for one's wrongs, and making memories were all valuable. But the lesson I cherished the most is realizing I was not and am not more important than anyone else. I am also no less important than anyone else. In the end, it has always been up to me to make a difference in the lives of others, just like my dad did for me.

Thank you, Dad!

Robin Helmuth

8

LESTER T. HERSHEY

Lester Hershey was born on November 28, 1912, in Youngstown, Ohio. He grew up in Argentina, where his parents were missionaries with the Mennonite Board of Missions. He went to Puerto Rico in 1947, where he served as director and the voice of the Luz y Verdad (Light and Truth) Spanish broadcast for more than 30 years. He was also the pastor of the Betania (Pulguillas) church and planted the churches in La Plata, Rabanal, Coamo, Coamo Arriba, and Pedro García. He served as an overseas mission worker in Puerto Rico, Mexico, and Spain and as a pastor in Chicago, Illinois; Pinto, Maryland; Washington, D.C.; and Martinsburg, Pennsylvania. He also served as an evangelist in several Latin American countries. He passed away on November 3, 2007.

———⊙———

I t is an honor and privilege to be able to share some thoughts on the life of my brother and pastor Lester Hershey. Not only is it a privilege, but standing behind a pulpit from which he spoke so many times gives me pause and causes me to tremble. To speak about a great servant of God named Lester Hershey is not an easy task, so I will talk a little bit about my own experiences. I have a few stories and anecdotes I'd like to share, appreciating at the same time that there are many, many more that could be told about him by many others.

I learned to know Pastor Hershey when I was a young boy. That circumstance came about because he made me work. The setting was a Summer Bible school. In an effort to gain more young people for the cause of Christ, Pastor Hershey offered a free Bible to anyone who would memorize all the verses he gave them. There were five of us who took up the challenge; and all five of us were able to memorize every one of the verses which he had given us. So it wasn't just one Bible we took from him at the end of vacation Bible school that summer, it was five. That was the summer of 1950. Of those five young people who earned a Bible that summer, sadly I am the only one who has remained faithful to the Lord, who has persevered to this date.

A servant of God is not ashamed of who he is, nor is it difficult to recognize him as such. That is the theme of what I want to speak about this afternoon. Brother Hershey lived in Pulguillas while pastoring the Betania church. Every Sunday afternoon he would get on a horse and, with a couple other members of the church, ride the twenty-five-minute trip to an outpost he had started called Coamo Arriba. The only way to reach that community was by foot or by horse, if you were fortunate enough to own one.

One day he got in his Jeep and started driving. He drove for an hour and twenty minutes, coming close to the point from where he had started. He then parked the vehicle and walked another hour and a half. During that walk, he walked past our house. He greeted my mother, Doña Rafaela, who "happened" to be home that day. My mother had been very, very sick. She had skin cancer, or melanoma, and it covered her face from one ear to the other. Brother Hershey, making it a point to always find ways to serve those who were in need, tried to persuade her to go to a clinic in Coamo Arriba, which was held every Tuesday afternoon by a doctor and/or a nurse from the Mennonite Hospital. It would be the closest medical attention she would find. But her answer was a firm "NO." Hershey was a stranger, she explained to me, her son. She didn't know who he was or where he was from. All she knew was that he was *un Americano.* Why should she listen to or trust him? So Hershey wasn't able to meet the objective of establishing what he considered a successful contact the first time around.

But Brother Hershey, who was a man of strong character and firm convictions, supplemented by a strong determination, decided that he would wait two weeks and then return. He spent a lot of time praying during those two weeks. Again my mother was home and he disarmed her with small chit-chat for a few moments, then told her about Christ. But my mother told him quite firmly, "I have my own religion, so don't you worry about it. They sent me home to die because there is no hope."

My mother, Doña Rafaela, not being able to forget Hershey's words, then sought advice from her godmother, and against her advice, decided to go to the clinic after all; but it was more out of curiosity as to who these people were rather than any hope of receiving help. (I should insert here that my mother was the religious leader for the Catholic Church in her community of Pedro García).

She walked the thirty minutes or so from her home to where the clinic was being held in Coamo Arriba, received a thorough check from the physician, and upon his recommendation decided to accept the offer of surgery to remove the cancer from her face.

And so it was that in the Mennonite Hospital, in a far-away community named La Plata, she received double healing; she received healing from her cancer and healing for her soul through the forgiveness of sins. She accepted Christ as her personal Savior and Lord. Defying all odds, she went on to live another 25 years after that surgery, turning her home into a scriptural Bethany. It became a place where visiting preachers and other Christian servants were always welcome. Few Sunday afternoons passed but what Brother Hershey and/or members of his family would not stop by for a meal of rice and beans, or at least, *un cafecito* (a cup of coffee).

It has been my observation that true servants of God do not wait to be called; rather, they go out seeking ways they can serve others. Pastor Hershey, as we lovingly called him—although he preferred that we call him simply Brother—left irreplaceable footprints in the island of Puerto Rico. Thanks to him and others who came after him we have in Puerto Rico a growing church that has not forgotten that one of their primary missions is to serve those who are in need—in the name of Jesus.

And not only that, I can say without fear of being contradicted that besides members from our churches pastors of many other denominations bear witness to the tremendous spiritual knowledge and growth seen as people completed the Bible correspondence courses offered by the radio broadcast program Luz y Verdad, which brother Hershey founded and led for many years.

The Bible says in Psalms 116:15, "Precious in the sight of the Lord is the death of His saints." And in Revelations 14:13 it says, ". . . Blessed are the dead who die in the Lord . . . Yes, says the Spirit, 'that they may rest from their labors, and their works follow them.'"

I would challenge all of you to listen to the last message Pastor Hershey gave. That day he quoted one of his favorite verses, "There is a season, or a time, for everything". It had a lot to say about his happiness, his joys and his opportunities, and even about some the tribulations and afflictions which some of us brought on him. I confess that I brought some of them on him, but he was quick to reconcile and forgive. He had a firm character. He was certain of his convictions and he never stopped being a sensible and compassionate person. He always seemed to understand completely every situation. The Spirit of God was upon him.

Then there were those who tried to pull a fast one or two on him, but that seldom worked. I remember well the story that a man, who was a heavy smoker, told me. Over the course of their friendship he learned that Pastor Hershey didn't approve of smoking. One day Brother Hershey went to visit him and found him smoking in the front yard of his house; although the man didn't know Hershey had seen him. Hershey had come up on him so fast the man hadn't had time to get rid of his stogie. So he quickly put it in his pocket. Hershey, wondering how it had disappeared so quickly, continued talking to him. Soon Brother Hershey saw some smoke coming out of the man's pocket, so he said to the man, "Friend, you better get that cigar out of your pocket or your pants will go up in flames!" THAT was Brother Hershey!

On another occasion we were having a service in one of the churches. We soon came to "that" time—the time to take up the tithes and offerings. As the offering plate was being passed, one of the men stood up and pulled a handkerchief out of his pocket. It had something in it and had all four corners tied together in a knot. As the man struggled to get the knot untied, he began telling the people sitting around him in a loud enough voice for most everyone to hear, "I won this money last night gambling." Hearing this comment, Pastor Hershey told me he determined not to say anything, although he did get quite red in the face! But . . . patience! It was another gift Pastor Hershey had developed over years of working with people. Later on Hershey spoke with the man, explaining to him why it wasn't right first of all to gamble and then to give the winnings to the church with the hope that this would absolve him. The man, realizing he'd "done wrong," went back to the church and, on his own, got up and apologized to the congregation for what he had done. He never gambled again. That was Hershey!

Hershey had a little bit of daring-do built into him as well. Most of the time he kept it in check, but sometimes it came in handy. Once upon a time, as the story goes, he filled a bus with men from the men's Bible study and prayer group from the church. Their mission was to go to different places around the island handing out tracts. Things went well; many tracts were given out to people they'd met, but soon it was time for them to eat. They saw a little roadside hangout and decided to stop there, as they hadn't seen any eating joints for some time.

The place was full of people and, to top it off, there was a juke box blaring some music quite loudly. What to do? Hershey went inside, sought out the owner, and said to him, "We want to eat here, but we really don't want to be listening to that loud music coming from the juke box. So tell me, how much money can you make from the juke box in two-hour's worth of continual playing? We will pay you for the income lost if you will keep the juke box quiet while we eat our lunch." The proprietor agreed. So the men got out of the bus, ordered their lunch, and while waiting for it started passing out the remaining tracts they had brought along to the people gathered there. Not only that, but when the patrons appeared receptive to this, Hershey got up and preached a good evangelistic message of salvation through Christ. That was Hershey!

One more quick anecdote, this one about a dialogue in the dark. One night brother Hershey and another preacher who had come down from the United States to visit were riding their horses back to Pulguillas (where Hershey lived), from Coamo Arriba, the same outpost referenced earlier where my mother had received medical treatment. They had been there, once again, to help in the weekly clinic held every Tuesday. Following that, the visiting pastor had shared the gospel in the little cinder block church built with blocks that had been carried, four at a time, tied on the backs of mules, down the steep trail to the building site.

By the time the service was over it was dark; but no fear, the horses could see very well at night, Hershey assured the visitor. Knowing the trail well Brother Hershey took the lead, with his guest following behind on his horse. They were talking about different aspects of the mission work in Puerto Rico, with the guest asking questions and Hershey answering them, sometimes with a story thrown in to illustrate his point. Finishing one of his stories, Hershey waited for a response or another question, but there was none. He heard the horse behind him, but the silence caused him to turn around to see if all was well. The horse was there for sure, but no rider! Looking past the horse down to the bottom of the steep hill they had just negotiated, he could barely see in the dim moonlight the other pastor, walking up the horse trail, trying to catch up to them. The hill was so steep that the man had slid out of his saddle and off the back of his horse, and Hershey, so involved in the story he was telling, hadn't heard the man fall off. Hershey got on the other horse, went back down the hill and helped the man back onto the horse. He walked behind them all the way back to the top of the hill, lest another calamity beset them. That was Hershey!

We could spend a long time telling stories about Brother Hershey and the people he led to the Lord in Puerto Rico. There are many, many people who, when they see or talk about Hershey, will invariably say, "That man is my father; that man is my spiritual father because he was the very first person to tell me about Jesus Christ and the salvation He offers. Hershey is the one who led me to the Lord."

Hershey was not only the first one to bring the gospel message to many of us, but he was also the first one to teach us the significance of being saved and how to daily walk and grow in the Lord. There were a great number of us who received salvation through his ministry and also his teachings of how to integrate the gospel into our daily living. He taught us how to be witnesses in both the things we said as well as how we lived our lives. He brought many of the leaders and pillars of the first generation church to the Lord. Here are the names of just a few of them: Don Pepe Santiago, Don Pablo González, Don Aurelio Bonilla, Don Cisco Delgado, Don Cendo Alvarado, and Don Juan Colón. These men were all led to the Lord by Brother Hershey and discipled to become the first generation pillars of the Mennonite church in Puerto Rico. And when its story is written these names will be familiar to many.

So the question begs to be asked, "Why all this? How is it that all of this happened?" Let me assure you that Hershey could tell us why. Without hesitation he would tell you that it was because he gave his life to Jesus Christ at a very early age; and that putting his hand to the plow, he never looked back. He made it his first priority to serve Christ with everything he had. He determined to be faithful and committed to Him and in so doing, to understand and then meet the needs of his neighbor.

For us the challenge is to imitate the faith and example of those who live in that manner, who are imitators of Christ. The kingdom of God, and the extension thereof, is not yet complete. God still needs people He can count on to carry out the great commission and tell the good news to those who will be receptive to that saving and healing grace found only in Jesus Christ.

Pastor Hershey was sure that one day the welcome mat would be extended to him upon reaching his heavenly homeland. How sure are you of that? Will you be extended that welcome mat when that time in your life arrives? This implies more than mere belief. It implies that it is not just believing but also following Jesus; not just saying it, but showing it with actions, with how you live your life.
My hope is that the Spirit of the Lord will be with each of us as we strive to be imitators of Christ in the same manner that Brother Lester Hershey did.

Enrique Ortiz
Message delivered at Lester Hershey's funeral

T he first time I had the pleasure of meeting Lester Hershey was in 1955 when I was barely eight years old. Everyone seemed to know this icon of the Mennonite work in Puerto Rico, but I did not know him personally since my family had just recently begun to attend the Mennonite church in La Plata. Mr. Hershey at that time was pastor of the Pulguillas church, and he and his family lived in the parsonage on the grounds. That day, though, my father had a school board meeting in Pulguillas, and while the adults were talking business, my sister and I had the fun of playing with the three Hershey children in their home. From this time on I felt comfortable in his presence, and as I had more opportunities to observe him in action I was impressed by his fluency in Spanish, his genuine smile, and his inexhaustible energy within our denomination and its outreach. His skill as an auctioneer at the classic Mennonite Church auction on Thanksgiving Day fascinated

44

me. In addition, I always loved to be near his beautiful horses, Snorty and Estrella, which he would use to visit the barrio of Coamo Arriba to minister.

Due to our age difference, the opportunities were few for sharing directly with this pioneer of Mennonite broadcasting on the Island. There was one event, though, I remember very clearly. It was a professional baseball game in Caguas between the Criollos de Caguas and the Senadores de San Juan. Hershey drove us there. It was a carful of noisy kids, which included his son and several of our friends and classmates. Everyone supported the Criollos de Caguas team, except me! I was sitting next to Hershey as we went to the game and noticed that he could not fully bend his arm. Unabashedly curious, I asked him about it, and he told me that while serving as a relief worker during the Spanish Civil War (1936-39) he had been shot in his arm, causing him this inflexibility. (Interesting to me years later, while doing research for a writing project of my own, I found articles about him in relation to this very event.)

I will always remember Hershey's kindness on this special day. Not only did he take us excited boys to that well-anticipated baseball game, but afterwards he took us to an ice cream shop in Caguas that was located across from the plaza! Not only did this place offer a wonderful assortment of Island-style *mantecado* with all its typical flavors, but was a favorite hangout for the professional baseball players themselves. Embedded in my memory I see myself, a short olive-skinned, curly-headed boy licking an ice cream cone, looking up, way up, at a tall, very tall, African American player surrounded by a bunch of people. It was Earl Wilson, a tall, strong Major League pitcher who was playing for the Criollos de Caguas that winter. Thanks to my friend's dad, I had that opportunity and that privilege that I will never forget!

Later, as an adult, I was fortunate to share more closely with Lester Hershey, and I personally experienced his support and his appreciation for what I was doing. While I was studying for my doctorate at the University of Iowa, Hershey contacted me to suggest I do some writing for the Puerto Rican magazine *Alcance Menonita*. This effort on his part encouraged me to continue writing then and afterwards.

A number of years later, during my first sabbatical from Goshen College in 1989-90, our paths crossed again. Lester, now widowed and retired, had returned to the Island to pastor the church in Pulguillas again. By that time I had done some research and writing on the history of the Mennonite church in the Spanish-speaking world, and Lester invited me to speak on this theme to his congregation. It was an interesting topic for me and a very personal subject for him: his father T.K. Hershey had been one of the pioneers of the Spanish-speaking Mennonite work in 1917 in Argentina. Like father like son, Lester T. Hershey has been indisputably a strong pillar of the Mennonite work in Puerto Rico.

Rafael Falcón

L ester had a unique presentation and reached out to all who listened to his messages. Each message had music relating to the topic and was very inspirational. Messages for "Corazón a Corazón" (Heart to Heart) were prerecorded in Argentina and sent to Aibonito, where the program was assembled with music and announcements. Prayer requests were sent from Argentina as well.

Lester was instrumental in coordinating the local Billy Graham crusade activities. Key pastors from Puerto Rico, South and Central America and the United States would visit the studio and record messages and music to be broadcast—what a blessing! Luz y Verdad under Lester's guidance coordinated sound systems in Cayey during pre-campaign activities. We were privileged to attend the crusade at Hiram Bithorn stadium during the main event as well.

Lester's home was on a small farm near Aibonito—complete with a cow or two! Always enjoyed a visit there on occasion!

Roger Studer

S omething was different that November afternoon in 2007, when my daughter, Julie, and I drove up the hill just outside of the town of Fort Ashby, West Virginia, got out of the car and walked into Daddy's house.

46

It wasn't the roads we had driven for the last 27 years or so that had changed. As we always did while driving the five hour trek from Richmond, Virginia, to Fort Ashby, West Virginia, we had commented about the hilliness of what we called the "Slanesville Cutoff". The road was winding, steep and quite narrow at places, causing cars to slow down considerably when encountering another one, lest one or the other be forced into the bank on one side, or over the edge on the other. Some might even call it a one-lane road, but the "Slanesville Cutoff" reduced the driving time for the trip by almost half an hour, and that was deemed enough to make the drive over Puerto Rico-like roads worthwhile. Besides, there were the traditional landmarks we had all come to look forward to which served as progress markers along the way.

And so, once again, we had come by the place where, as little girls, my daughters had dubbed an open field on the side of a hill with a small, solitary house in the middle of it, "The Little House on the Prairie." Over the years, we had watched as the little house had grown substantially in size and a small barn had been built to house the livestock, whose sole duty was to see that the grass in the field was maintained at a respectable height.

We had come over "Julie's Mountain," named thus because this was the point where a young Julie would invariable begin asking, "Are we there yet, are we there yet?"

And finally there was the little white chapel, an old-timey sort, with a tall steeple and windows that arched to a point at the top. After a particular rough time in my life, I was traveling to Daddy's place hoping for some encouragement.

It had been dusk, the wintery wind was cold and snowflakes were dancing in the air as they meandered their way down to the ground. As I came up on the chapel, sitting there in front of the old cemetery, I noticed that the lights were on and they were having a pre-Christmas service. It was an "Ideals Magazine" moment.

I had pulled into the parking lot and, despite the cold wind and snow, sat there with the window rolled down, taking it all in. Then, I got out of my car and slipped into one of the back pews. Several families, enough to fill about half of the chapel, were hearing a message of hope for a world that was in need; and I, at that moment, needed it as much, if not more, than they did.

Every trip, these places, and their accompanying stories would be duly recounted, even if those little girls were now young adults with lives of their own. But being captives in the car with me, they, or anyone else, had little choice but to hear it all once again!

We got out of the car, walked up the sidewalk to his house, opened the front door and walked in; just as we had done so many times over the past years. Our eyes were instantly drawn to the maroon-colored, leather recliner on the other side of the living room . . . and it was empty! We both knew it would be, yet we both wished it wouldn't have been. We wanted to see Daddy put down the newspaper, magazine or book he'd be reading, get up from his recliner and say with a smile, "Well, I guess you made it, huh?" Then he'd walk over and give each of us a hug and ask about how the trip had gone.

That's what was different about this trip! We had gotten in the same car, traveled the same roads, carried on conversations that were reminiscent of others we'd had and walked into the same house. The difference was that this time, Daddy wasn't there. The Lord, whom he had served faithfully for seventy or more years, had come by a few days earlier and had told him it was time; time to go to his *real* home and receive his eternal reward.

These are the times when we find ourselves taking a pause to reflect on what a life, truly dedicated to God and His service, is capable of accomplishing. And so that night, after everyone else had gone to bed, I got up, went out into the living room, sat down in Daddy's recliner, leaned back with feet propped up, and in the quiet darkness of that night, I began to remember.

I remembered how he had told me that his dad, Tobias Kreider Hershey—T.K. they called him—had been a hardware store employee when he heard the call from God to go and share the Gospel to those who hadn't heard. He responded, left it all behind, and he, his wife Mae, daughter Beatrice and Lester (my dad), had boarded a ship to Argentina in 1916, my dad being four years old. The T.K. Hersheys and the J.W. Shenks were the first two missionaries the Mennonite church had decided to send to Latin America, and both families ended up in Argentina.

He never spoke too much about his growing up years there, but he must have enjoyed sports and experienced at least a moderate degree of success. I've seen pictures of him leading the pack in a foot race at school; another photo showed him playing on the soccer field, ball between his feet, looking up to plot his next move, and Grant Stoltzfus, professor at Eastern Mennonite University when I was a student there, told me that my Dad was unstoppable in the soccer games they used to play at Goshen College.

But Daddy was also impressed with the long distances between towns in the Northern Pampas, the few dirt roads available and the very tiring train rides Grampa Hershey would come back from. There is also a picture of a young teenage Lester standing beside a car stuck up to its axles in mud, a not uncommon situation in those days.

He also was, apparently, quite "musically inclined." He loved to sing, and developed a quite acceptable base voice. More importantly, he studied piano and became quite good at it; a skill that helped him in his later years as a missionary in Puerto Rico. I loved to hear him play the old termite-infested piano in our house. He could play by ear, and it was great music when he wasn't bound by the notes on the paper. He often played in the young churches when nobody else was around who could. We had a small pump organ that was somewhat portable and I can remember pulling it out of the back of the car or Jeep, carrying it into the home or church where the service was about to begin, unfolding it, then reversing the task after the service had ended. There were many such times when he played, pumping away mightily, while at the same time leading or teaching a song.

As a young man he also became aware of the lack of publishing houses able or willing to print material that could be used in the growth of the church, such as tracts, Sunday school materials and Bible study supplies and other printed matter.

And so, early in his life, a plan, which he believed was from God, began to form in the back of his young mind. After finishing high school in Argentina, he would go back to the United States and attend college; he would then learn the trade of printing, and lastly, he would get his pilot's license. He would then go back to Argentina and set up a printing press that would meet the constant need for printed material. He would also take an airplane back with him, which he would use to negotiate the long distances between mission outposts, particularly in the Pampa regions in the north of the country.

I remembered him telling me—to my surprise—that the fact that not a single part of that "plan" had ever really come to fruition, had never really bothered him. Early in life he had learned that the road to being in God's will could be filled with all kinds of twists, turns, and bumps in the road; that the sooner a person learned and could accept that, the more satisfying and fulfilling life would be. In a nutshell, his view of God's leading amounted to the following: stay current on your Bible reading and prayer, church activities, etc.; honestly determine what your strengths and weaknesses are; and look for areas where you could work to sharpen them. Amazingly, as often as not, he told me, God would present areas of service where he felt he was weakest in, but he never shied away from them because he believed, and had experienced, that if God calls you to do something, He will also give you the strength, ability and desire to carry it out. Over and over, I heard him tell young Christians that if they saw a need, but weren't sure if God wanted them to fill it, start working in that direction, and if God didn't want you there, He would close the door, while opening a window in some other area. And more often than not, that window would grow to be greater in scope than what that door initially appeared to be.

He believed that God doesn't expect us to sit around for a "revelation" of His will; rather, look for opportunities, do your best to fill the need and God will make it abundantly clear if this is where He wants you. He often quoted Isaiah 30:21 which says, "… and you will hear a voice *behind* you saying, *this* is the way; walk ye in it' when you turn to the left or to the right." Daddy's guidelines for Christian witness, whether in ministry or secular world were simple: 1) Work, 2) Pray, 3) Wait. He worked as if everything depended upon him; he prayed as if everything depended upon God; and then he waited, knowing that the outcome would be what God allowed. These guidelines never failed him.

I remembered him saying that, upon returning to the United States in July of 1931, and after attending his sister's wedding to Will Hallman (they subsequently became missionaries in Argentina for over 50 years), he enrolled as a freshman at Goshen College.

While there, he began taking flying lessons. I still have a little booklet he had entitled "How to Fly a Piper Cub." His classes were full of as many Biblical studies as he could fit in. The "plan," as he understood it at that point, seemed to be working.

After graduating from Goshen College in 1936 he spent a year working at the Mennonite Publishing House in Scottsdale, Pennsylvania, where he learned the trade of printing. An interesting tidbit here is that, while working one of the printing presses, he somehow got his foot in the wrong place and the machine not only took part of his shoe but part of a toe on his right foot as well! After this, he attended Goshen Biblical Seminary, being a member of the Seminary's first graduating class in 1938 with a Th.B. degree.

Then came the first "bump in the road." It was the mid-1930s and Europe was in great turmoil. Hitler had secured total power and was flexing his muscles in direct opposition to the terms of surrender imposed on Germany after the Great War. General Francisco Franco was trying to gain power in Spain by overthrowing the popularly-elected government of the Second Spanish Republic, while Germany was looking for an opportunity to test its newly developed military equipment and strategies. Hitler offered military assistance, and General Franco accepted. Soon Spain was inundated with German military advisers and new military equipment and her long tentacles could be found everywhere in Spain.

It was during this time of civil war that Daddy was asked by the Mennonite Central Committee (M.C.C.) if he would pray about going to Spain and helping in the relief work they had established there. Yes he would, Daddy responded, after praying about it. So it wasn't long before he found himself boarding a ship on his way to

France, and from there to Spain.

As a boy, I was always fascinated by his "Spain stories." Two incidents stand out in my mind and are worth recounting. Organizations carrying out relief work were required to register before beginning activity in a given area. When Daddy went into the municipal building to present the paperwork, he found a German officer sitting at the desk. After being questioned "rather severely" (Daddy's words), the German officer told him that he believed Daddy to be a Jewish spy and promptly proceeded to put him in jail. It took a couple of days for the "misunderstanding" to be cleared up, but it was long enough for my Dad to be able to understand, at least to a small degree, what other political prisoners were facing and having to live through. Many of their stays ended with a visit to the firing squad rather than being released.

The other incident was one whose mark he carried for the rest of his life. They used a delivery truck or van to transport the supplies they were distributing. As is the case during wartime, multiple checkpoints were set up on the roads to control the comings and goings of the citizens of the country. Daddy was quite used to them by this time, and the guards working the checkpoints were familiar with the markings on the side of the M.C.C. delivery trucks, to the point of often not requiring them to completely stop to show their paperwork. Typically, the guard would see the vehicle, signal for it to stop, and then seeing it was the relief distribution truck wave it on through.

This particular day had started out like any other. Daddy had helped load the supplies to be distributed, got into the truck and started down the road. He soon came upon his first checkpoint. Seeing the guard signal for him to stop, he began to slow the truck, downshifting so the motor would help brake the loaded truck for the stop. The guard, recognizing the distribution vehicle as the relief supplies carrier that it was, motioned Daddy to go on through. Seeing the guard's signal, he began speeding up again, shifting gears as he picked up speed. He remembers looking back in his side mirror and seeing another soldier come out of the guardhouse, kneel down on one knee, aim at the truck and fire. Daddy was in the process of shifting gears, thus his hand was on the truck's floor shifter. The noise from the rifle and the searing pain that shot up his arm were almost simultaneous. He stopped the truck as quickly as he could, and soon the guards were there, pulling him out. Had the bullet traveled a mere six inches more to the left, the story would most likely have had a far different ending.

Holding his arm as the pain grew, he looked at the guard and asked, "Why?" The guard simply answered, "You didn't stop." Simple question, simple answer! So Daddy, still alert enough to know that you don't argue with the man who holds the gun and already has shot you once, said no more. His arm was bleeding profusely, as an artery had been severed, and bones, like little pieces of shrapnel, were splattered everywhere. His right elbow had been shattered and he needed medical attention—right now.

I remembered Daddy telling me that he just about died that day; not because of the injury (many people, unfortunately, lose a limb in war), but because of all the blood he had lost before they could get him the proper medical attention. Ultimately he was taken to France, where a surgeon told him he'd never have use of his arm again. "Your elbow was so shattered I just started tying nerve ends together randomly, and I used the cupped palm of my hand to form a kind of elbow at an angle that would allow you to at least put your hand in your pocket. But don't expect any movement. Many of your elbow's bones are shattered or missing." The surgeon arranged Daddy's thumb so it pointed in towards his bent fingers. "That way", the surgeon explained, "maybe you can at least recover some coins out of your pocket". They gave him a small rubber ball to place between his fingers and the palm of his hand and told him to work on squeezing it as often as he could. But they offered no hope that he'd ever regain use of his elbow, hand or fingers.

A sidebar to the above is that God restored the use of his hand to the extent that he was able to write and type, but his elbow only achieved a few degrees of movement, so that things which most men do without giving it a second thought required an extra effort and/or dexterity. Things like buttoning his shirt, tying his necktie, threading his belt and even blowing his nose were a one-handed operation. Eating required a spoon with a long stem on it or using his left hand. I tried doing these things on occasion and gained a new respect for his never complaining.

Back in the United States again—it was April, 1940—he refused to let grass grow under his feet. There were ducks he needed to get lined up in order to prepare for shipping to Argentina and, just as importantly, a certain young woman he had been corresponding with while in Spain had his interest.

Alta Evalena Good had grown up on a farm near Fisher, Illinois, the eighth of nine children born to Peter and Mary Good. The first person to attend college from her community in central Illinois, she studied to became a teacher. After graduating she accepted a teaching position in a one-room country school house, teaching all the elementary grades simultaneously.

But her *real* love was farming, and her only dream in life was to become a farmer's wife and live out her life on a farm. Little could she imagine the life that was in store for her that summer day in June, 1941, when she said "I do" in a wedding held at her brother Roy's farmhouse not too far from the town of Rantoul in central Illinois. She would, indeed, be helping her husband with the planting and harvesting of the seed, but it would be a far different seed from the corn and soy beans she had helped her father and brothers plant during her growing up years.

By this time (summer of 1941), World War II had grown into a war worthy of its name, and the second "bump in the road" emerged. Because the German submarines made traveling by ship to Argentina unsafe, Daddy and Mother were asked if they would take over a ministry in Chicago among the Spanish-speaking Mexican migrant workers and other Latinos living in the city. They prayed about it. And once again, without hesitation, they said "yes." (I remember my Dad telling me that he was reluctant to accept the "order" from the Mennonite Mission Board, but he remembered what he had learned from his dad, T.K. Hershey; always respond in the affirmative to the Church's wishes unless there is an obvious reason not to). They moved into a third floor apartment located in an old building that housed a necktie factory on the first floor and the "meeting place" on the second.

The next five or so years brought great joy to them as they watched the Lord more than double the size of the church and forged friendships that lasted a lifetime. It was also during these years that all three of their children, two girls and a boy, were born.

These years in Chicago were years of training and personal growth which he couldn't have easily gotten anywhere else. He organized the church into a congregation separate from the Home Mission. He was successful in developing an effective program in evangelism. Sunday services became bi-lingual in the morning while remaining Spanish-only in the evenings. He became quite active in the Illinois Mennonite Conference, where he was asked to assume several positions of leadership, and he developed and led a summer camp program for underprivileged boys from the inner city of Chicago. But years later he wrote that "even with all the blessings and opportunities they gave me, and as much as I felt at home with my Mexican brethren and leaders of the Illinois Mennonite Conference, I still couldn't shake off the 'feeling' that I needed to return to Argentina."

Then, as most wars do, World War II finally came to an end in Europe in 1945, and traveling to Argentina once again became the focus for the Hersheys. The Mennonite Board of Missions agreed that it would be a good thing for them to finally head to Argentina, where Daddy would begin working out the plans he felt God had placed on his heart. Consequently, the Board purchased four tickets (I wouldn't be born until December of the following year), and made arrangements for the Hersheys to travel.

Bump in the road number three! Juan Domingo Perón, the Argentine dictator, had issued an order that no foreigner could live in Argentina who did not have an I.D. indicating he/she had lived there before he came into power. Thinking this a no-brainer because of the fifteen years he had spent there as a youth, Dad began looking for his I.D. But try as he might, he could not find it, and without it he knew living in Argentina was out of the question. Attempts by the missionaries already there to secure a duplicate had failed. So the four tickets, which had been sought after by the

Hersheys for so many years, were ultimately taken by Clifford and Doris Snyder and their two children, Margaret and Arnold. Sadly, Clifford died on the ship and was buried at sea.

During the war the U.S. government had made allowance for conscientious objectors to work in some form of alternate service instead of serving in the military. Some of the possibilities were working in community development, agriculture, or medical work in various parts of the country. Puerto Rico, being a commonwealth of the U.S., had been approved for this type of government service.

It was only natural that the life and witness of these conscientious objectors would have an effect on the people with whom they were working. This being the case, it wasn't long before the Mennonite Board of Missions determined that the situation was ripe for the expansion of their witness into one of church planting and growth.

"Bump in the road" number four! Returning from a meeting the Mission Board had just held, S.C. Yoder, President of the Board, asked my parents if they would be willing to delay their South America plans to begin a mission work in La Plata, Puerto Rico. "But what about Argentina?" my Dad asked them. "We're only talking about a two-year commitment," they replied. "Go to Puerto Rico for two years, then take a much deserved six month vacation. After that, we'll talk Argentina again. The paperwork problems should be a thing of the past and you should be able to travel to Argentina without further obstacles."

After praying about it, my parents agreed, and it wasn't long before the five Hersheys boarded the three-tailed Eastern Airlines Super Constellation in Miami and headed for San Juan, P.R. It was only a four hour flight, but it would be a totally different world. The month was March, the year was 1947 and the three littlest Hersheys, Janice Jo, Sherilyn Mae and Lester Eugene, were ages 4, 2 and 4 months, respectively.

The "reception committee" that had traveled to the military airport on Isla Grande to welcome us was made up of old friends Dr. George Troyer and his wife Kathryn, Elmer and Clara Springer (whom my mother had grown up with in central Illinois), Paul and

Lois Lauver and a few others. It was also very hot—high 90s and high humidity.

They fell in love with Puerto Rico and the people living there almost immediately. Daddy quickly threw himself into visitation, handing out tracts and inviting people to come to the *culto* or services that were held several times a week.

One such day he was returning to the parsonage he had built beside the church and two young boys stopped him and asked, "Is your Sunday night service in the church here open to anyone who wants to attend?". Surprised by the question, yet recognizing an opportunity when God presented it, he told them that the services held at the church were open to everyone and gave them a special invitation to come the following Sunday. They came the next Sunday, and the following Wednesday night for Bible study, and the following Sunday morning and every other time the church doors were open. It wasn't long before these high school age cousins gave their life to Christ.

Their names were Fidel and Miguel Santiago. From the very beginning Fidel threw himself enthusiastically into learning all he could about the Lord, reading his Bible and patterning his life from what he read and learned. He grew up to be a highly respected leader in the church, married Patricia Brenneman, a teacher in the school at the time, and among many other things served as pastor of the church in Cayey and the announcer for the radio broadcast Luz y Verdad, which my dad directed for many years.

And Miguel? Well, it was a little longer road for him. He married and moved away. Years later, he, his wife and two sons returned to La Plata where they began classes preparing them for baptism. While Daddy was no longer the pastor there, he had the privilege of returning and completing the circle by baptizing both Miguel and his wife.

It didn't take Daddy long, however, to figure out that he'd make better use of his time if he had a horse, and so he bought one— "Barney." My mother invariable accompanied him on these visitation trips, something she continued to do during their entire ministry, and in fact, as Daddy's responsibilities grew, she would often go out visiting by herself.

Due to the post-war boom that was taking place in the U.S., many families found themselves in need of more than one car, thus the "two-car family" become a common term used in describing them. During that time in Puerto Rico, however, cars were not as useful as horses for getting around in the rural areas, so it wasn't long before the Hersheys became a two-horse family.

Daddy always sought to take other people from the church to help out with the teaching, song leading, scripture reading, etc. whenever he went somewhere. He felt it was a way to encourage growth in the young Christians and a way of helping them understand that witnessing to others was not just the pastor's job but something each Christian should feel comfortable doing as part of their spiritual growth. Consequently, he would seek out those he felt had the potential to become future leaders and mentored them as they would assume more and more responsibilities.

One of the men who had recently accepted Christ as his Savior was Don Juan Colón. My earliest memory of Don Juan and his wife Doña Celina was when I went with Daddy to the Rabanal church house for a service. There were quite a few horses tied down outside, and one by one their owners would mount them and head home.

Then, I saw something I had never seen before in my young life. A man got one of the horses and led it to his waiting wife. She got on, after which the man lifted a small girl to sit in front of her on the horse's back and another young girl to sit behind her. I thought, "Wow, three people on a horse." So imagine my surprise when this same man then went for another horse, mounted it, and proceeded to pull up two young boys he sat behind him and two more who found a seat in front of him—five on a horse!

The man's name, of course, was Juan Colón and his wife Celina. They became two of the earliest members of the Rabanal church, and this was how they came and left each time they attended a service. Over the years, not only were they faithful in attendance and helped out extensively in the church, they became good friends of my parents, and one of their sons, Benjamín, and I, who were in the same grade, went through school together from third grade through high school. The Lord blessed Juan Colón's commitment to Him and prospered him greatly in his agricultural and chicken raising businesses over the years. And among many other leadership roles, Don Juan served as pastor of the Rabanal church for some time.

All of that to say that it was Juan Colón who made it possible for us to become a two-horse family, as Daddy bought "Rex" from him soon after they had first met.

So it wasn't long before 'Barney' became "Alta's horse," and any time she needed to go somewhere Barney was the horse to take her there. He had a very smooth "pace," and my mom loved riding him. He also developed a reputation of being the horse that loved lying down in the water whenever they crossed the La Plata River (there was no bridge that spanned the river at that point), leaving his unsuspecting rider quite wet at times! That, of course, unless my Mom was on his back. Growing up on the farm where handling horses was one of the first things she had learned (this was before steam engines and tractors became common), ol' Barney would be on his best behavior whenever she was on his back. Horses have a way of understanding rather quickly who the boss is, and it only took a single attempt at laying down in the water for Barney to quickly learn that my mom was the boss indeed!

My memories of our early years in La Plata are somewhat vague, but I distinctly remember one Friday night. I must have been in the third or fourth grade. It was around 10:30 at night. All three of we kids had long since gone to bed and my folks had just crawled under the covers. Suddenly, we were all awakened by a loud knocking on the door. It scared me because it sounded like a very urgent knocking, not one where somebody wanted to come visit for a while but had failed to notice just how late it really was. By the time my Dad had jumped out of bed and had quickly slipped on some clothes, the urgent knock had repeated itself several times, and the knocker had begun calling out to Daddy; "Pastor, Pastor"!

Daddy opened the door to a young man who, by all appearances, had been running hard and was quite out of breath. He was still trying to catch it. In spite of his heavy breathing, he was able to blurt out his mission: Don Víctor Rivera was at the local bar and had gotten very drunk, and in the process was saying all sorts of things that he never would say when sober. Daddy had had the privilege of leading Don Víctor, normally a quiet man and of a gentle spirit, to the Lord early on after we had arrived in La Plata and he had been one of the persons in the first group of believers Daddy had baptized. But he had struggled mightily against the "bottle," and the trend of the line on the graph, after an initial upward trajectory, had leveled off and maybe had even begun a downward turn. The enemy was using Don Víctor's weakness to dampen his otherwise good testimony in the community.

Daddy quickly found the keys to the Willys Jeep and headed for the garage. I asked if I could go along, fully not expecting to be allowed to because of the lateness of the hour, but to my surprise he nodded his head yes. As I had already put on my clothes, I jumped into the back seat nestled between the two square aft wheel wells, while the young man climbed into the seat on the passenger's side up front.

We drove for about eight to ten minutes, at which point the young man asked to be let go. I assume he didn't want to be seen as the one who had "ratted" on Don Víctor. We continued on the winding, steep dirt road until we arrived. We got out, walked into the now empty one-room bar, and there was Don Víctor, sitting at a small table with a bottle of whiskey in one hand and a small glass in the other. His eyes were bloodshot, and when he saw Daddy, knowing he had been "caught" with his hand in the cookie jar, managed, with difficulty, to stand up, and with slurred speech, attempted a greeting.

Silently, Daddy went over to the table, took the partly filled glass of whiskey out of Don Víctor's hand and with his other grabbed the bottle and, walking over to the bartender, gave them both to him, all the time remaining silent. I, of course, wasn't allowed to go in, but standing just outside the door I managed to peak around the edge of it for the view of what was transpiring.

Daddy then went over to Don Víctor, who was standing there

open-mouthed, put his arm around his shoulders and began walking him out of the bar. He steered him to the Jeep, opened the metal tubing-framed canvas door and helped him in. By that time I was in the back seat, so we headed back down the steep hill. Finally Daddy spoke: "Don Víctor, do you know that God is very, very sad to see you in such a condition? He wants to help you, but you, too, need to make an *esfuerzo*—an effort—to give up the bottle. I'm taking you to my house and we're going to pray until God gives you the victory." Don Víctor, with alcohol emanating from every pore of his body, was slouched over and could only mumble something unintelligible in response.

Arriving back at our house, Daddy helped Don Víctor into our kitchen and sat him down at the small table where we usually ate our meals. He made some strong, black coffee and served it to him. I don't know how many cups it took to sober him up, but while he was drinking them Daddy kept reminding him over and over how much God loved him and how sad He was tonight to see him in such a state.

Finally, in the wee hours of the morning, the coffee having rendered its intended effect of sobering up the man, Daddy asked if he was ready to turn everything over to God, including (or maybe especially) his weakness for alcohol. Daddy again put his arm around his shoulders and began praying. Then Don Víctor prayed, stopping occasionally to cover his face with his hands in a vain attempt to hold back the sobs. He asked God to forgive him for not trusting Him more, and he kept saying over and over again, "I don't want to drink any more. Please, Jesus, take it (the desire to drink) away from me. Take it away from me."

After Don Víctor prayed in this manner for a while, Daddy again prayed for him. When he finished, Don Víctor stood up, wiped his eyes with the clean handkerchief Daddy had offered him and began to smile. It was what is better known as an "ear-to-ear" grin, and he kept saying over and over as he walked around the kitchen, "*¡Pastor, me lo quitó! ¡Gracias Señor! ¡Me lo quitó!*" (Pastor, He took it away! Thank you, Lord! He took it away!")

And so it was that early on a Saturday morning I was witness to

God's healing power in taking away an unwanted habit from a man who earnestly sought God's help. This was Don Víctor's testimony; that from that day forward he never touched another drop of alcohol, nor did he ever again crave for it.

It was while the church building in Rabanal was under construction that Daddy and Elmer Springer, a builder/engineer type in charge of the Mission building projects, had an experience they both would chuckle about when retelling the incident.

Pulguillas, the earliest church-planting effort in Puerto Rico, was where Elmer and Clara Springer lived. Because Puerto Rico was located right down "Hurricane Alley," it was decided early on that the mission buildings would be built out of cement blocks. They had a manually operated cement block machine that cranked out a whopping four blocks at a time. Sufficient mortar was mixed to fill the cavity with dividers to make four blocks. After it dried, a large handle was swung 180 degrees that would pull the forms away from the dried mortar, and four cement blocks would be stacked and more mortar would then be mixed. I remember playing with this machine when it was all rusty and abandoned, and we'd attempt to make blocks out of mud. But invariably the mud would collapse and we'd wonder off, looking for a more fulfilling adventure.

A stash of blocks, enough to build the one room church building in Rabanal, had been formed, so Daddy and Elmer began driving them to the construction site in an old International dump truck the Mission owned at the time. It was about an hour's drive and the roads were nothing more than dirt "sugar cane trails" that turned into mud when it rained.

A good tropical rain had fallen and, sure enough, the roads quickly turned into mud as Daddy and Elmer neared Rabanal. It wasn't long before they were stuck up to their axles in mud. As they sat there in the truck, weighing their options, it began to rain again. There was nothing they could do but wait for the rain to stop so they could go and find help.

Suddenly, a man came walking from what seemed out of nowhere, oblivious to the hard rain and muddy road. His old, worn, work clothes indicated that he was one of the laborers (*peones*) on the farm the road had been cut through, and he was soaked to the bone. He was wearing a *"pava"*, an old hat with its rims turned up and the ribbon around its base was shredded with age. Seeing the truck was stuck in the mud, he stopped to see if he could help these *americanos* in any way. Daddy thanked him for stopping and told him they'd most likely need a team of horses to pull them out once the rain stopped.

The man promised to tell the farm owner of their need for help and, meanwhile, he would go home and bring them some coffee to warm them up while they waited. The man left, but there was no let-up in the rain.

It wasn't long before the good Samaritan returned. In one hand he was carrying an old oatmeal can, long emptied of its oatmeal content and now filled to the top with steaming black coffee. To keep from burning his hand, he had wrapped corn husks around the outside of the can. In his other hand he balanced a couple cups and saucers stacked on top of each other. He poured the coffee into one cup and gave it to my Dad, who then passed it over to Elmer. As the man went to pour the remaining coffee into the other cup he was holding, he noticed there were a couple of corn silks inside the cup. He paused for a moment, embarrassed to see them there, then, without another thought, tipped his hat forward, enabling the water that had accumulated inside the turned up rim to flow into the cup. He swished it around a couple of times, then poured the water and silks out onto the ground. He then filled the cup with coffee and handed it to Daddy, who proceeded to drink it as they chit-chatted some more.

After a while the rain stopped and the man left, saying he would soon return with some horses and to pick up the cups and saucers. After the man left, Elmer looked at Daddy and laughingly said, "I'm sure glad I got the first cup of coffee!" They laughed some more while Daddy allowed as how the coffee was hot enough to most likely kill, or at least greatly discourage, any "cooties" that might have had some bad intentions. Soon the Samaritan returned with friends and several horses and they were able to pull the truck out of the mud hole.

Construction continued until the day arrived when they were able to check off the last "box." It was time to celebrate and thank God for another building finished that would be used to spread the Word and teach others about God's great love.

And so the day arrived. People came on horseback and on foot from La Plata, Pulguillas, the Baptist church in the nearby town of Cidra, and the Rabanal community. It was quite a celebration for a rural community such as Rabanal, and after the dedication a week of evangelistic meetings was planned in the new building.

But no success is achieved by God's people without the enemy throwing some roadblocks to try to discourage the Message from going out.

There was a new road being built from Cidra (the closest town) to Rabanal which was very helpful for the people needing to go to town for medical attention and business, but didn't help at all if you were trying to reach the place from La Plata. It was still by horse or by foot.

During that week of special meetings some people driving in from the Cidra side found large piles of rocks in the middle of the road requiring them to park their cars and walk the rest of the way. Another time the road grader was found to be parked across the road, blocking any further travel but by foot. And a young 12-year-old boy who had attended all the services and had accepted Christ into his life was told that when he died the devil would scratch his eyes out of his head. But the boy answered and said, "I don't care what happens to my body when I die. I will be in heaven with Jesus and I know the Devil isn't allowed in heaven! And anyway, I like what I hear and read from the Bible!"

And not long after that, Melquiades Santiago, one of the young men from La Plata Daddy had been mentoring, became the pastor of the Rabanal church.

Wednesday nights were Bible study nights at the new church. The ride up the hill from La Plata typically took Daddy around 35 minutes without stops, but along the way he usually would stop at homes to visit, give them tracts and invite them to the evening Bible study, so most Wednesdays he'd leave shortly after lunch.

He had mounted an old farm bell outside the church which he would always ring one hour before the starting time of 7:00 p.m. and again 30 minutes before starting time. Since the community had no electricity, they used two Aladdin pressure lamps to light the chapel.

Daddy had begun painting a Biblical text over the front wall, behind the pulpit. It read in Spanish, "Believe on the Lord Jesus Christ, and you will be saved" (Acts 16:31). After each service he'd stay and hand paint a few letters. Finally the day arrived when he had only five or six more letters to finish the project, so he told my mom that he was going to finish the lettering, thus he'd be home later than usual.

The service had ended and the people had left, so he turned his attention to the letters of the verse. Finishing, and happy with the results, he turned out the Aladdin lamps, locked the door behind him and headed towards the fence post where he had tied the rope that kept the horse from straying, but allowed him to eat some grass while waiting.

He followed the rope, expecting to find Barney at the end of it. But this night Barney wasn't where he was supposed to be—at the end of the rope. He found only an empty halter. (In later years, when Daddy talked about this, I used to kid him, saying that at that moment it took him awhile to figure out whether he had found a rope or lost his horse!) We always had a good laugh. But walking home over a steep foot trail really wasn't a laughing matter, although he had done it many times before pre-horse, and there was the river, and dogs, and stones to trip over on a moonless night. He wondered if this was another one of the enemies' tricks to make it a little tougher than it would need be. There was still some animosity from some "religious people" who weren't too happy with someone "infringing" on their "territory."

Since there wasn't anything else to do but start walking home, that is what he did, hoping he'd run across Barney on the way. As he approached a fork in the path that led to a small house, he remembered there was a very large dog that would always come out and grab hold of the horse's tail and just hang on to it for a distance, then let go. Daddy, not relishing the thought of a big dog hanging onto him in any form or fashion, began to pray; "Lord, I remember how you took care of Daniel in the lion's den, so I'm asking you to keep this dog away so I don't get bit." He kept on walking, and when he reached the short lane leading to the house there was no dog. A bit farther down the path the dog began to bark, but he never came anywhere close to where Daddy was, and he went on down the path, thanking the Lord for his protection.

Then, a little farther on, he remembered there was a large tobacco leaf-drying barn where some other young dogs hung out. The barn had no door, just a large opening through which people could leave or enter. These dogs would typically come out to meet the horses as they went by, barking their little heads off, while keeping their distance from the horse's hooves. Again Daddy prayed, "Lord, keep me safe from this pack of dogs as you did from the one earlier tonight." He kept on walking, and as he passed the large tobacco barn he could hear the dogs barking and carrying on inside, but not a single one came out of the barn as he passed by. Again he thanked God for sending an angel to keep the dogs from coming out that open door.

He soon found himself at the edge of the La Plata River. There was no bridge, so people normally waded through it at a couple shallow areas, providing it hadn't rained up river. If it had, the river could very quickly be turned into a deep, boiling and raging wall of water. When this happened the people just had to let it run its course until it returned to its normal tranquil self.

Tonight, though, the water was only about ankle deep. Still, it required bending over to take off shoes and socks and roll up ones pant legs to keep from getting any wetter than necessary. Completing the ritual, he walked across the river, and upon reaching the other side leaned over and did it all again. From there on the road was paved, although the term "paved" was used loosely in describing their condition, but compared to the dirt paths, it was a welcome change.

For no reason at all, he said, he touched his shirt pocket and instantly realized that the glasses he had put in there at the beginning of his walk from Rabanal were not there. He had just purchased them a few weeks earlier, having to wait for weeks while they were made, then shipped, from the U.S. mainland. Once again, he breathed a request; "Lord, You've done so much for me tonight already. But please keep them safe until I return tomorrow to look for the horse and help me find them as well. Thank you."

The next morning he was up early, hoping to find his glasses before an unsuspecting person could step on them and crush them. He saddled Rex and backtracked his route from the previous night. Reaching the river's edge, there on a flat rock were his glasses, all folded up and sitting as pretty as could be, and not a scratch on them. Overwhelmed with thanksgiving, he crossed the river, went a short distance and there was Barney, grazing on some grass right beside the path. He put a rope around him and led him home.

About this whole experience he wrote, "Was there ever any doubt that the Lord doesn't hear and answer prayer in even small practical matters? This served to strengthen my faith in the Lord and gave me another story to tell which illustrated His faithfulness and would bring glory to my Father. Praise His name!"

My parents' ministry in Puerto Rico could be described as having three distinct phases. The first phase was their outreach while based in La Plata; their second phase was their ministry while living in Pulguillas; and the third phase actually spanned both of the others: radio broadcasting.

We hadn't been in Puerto Rico even four months before Daddy got a quartet together, composed of the young men serving their alternate service, and drove to Ponce, a city on the southern coast of the island, to begin weekly broadcasts from the radio station WPAB. This ministry quickly grew parallel to their church planting and building ministry. By the late 1950s it had grown to the point where the broadcast, Audición Luz y Verdad (Light and Truth), could be heard in every Spanish speaking country in the world. While this became their principle focus, they never gave up pastoring a local church.

The above experiences of my parent's ministry, then, primarily reflects their "La Plata Days", and basically ignores the Luz y

Verdad and Pulguillas years of service. Believe me when I say that both of the other ministries could fill quite a bit more space than the selected ones above written about in their La Plata days of service. In a very real sense, those two other phases of service deserve much more attention than space in this venue could allow. Suffice it to say that their work for the Lord was blessed greatly in these two other fields of service as well.

And so it was that, after 37 years of service in Puerto Rico, Daddy and Mother "retired" back in the U.S. They built a house in Fort Ashby, close to where my oldest sister and husband lived with their four children. At the time, my other sister was living in Oregon and I was living in Perú, and then Bolivia, serving with Wycliffe Bible Translators as a missionary pilot.

But not even a year had passed before they were asked if they would go to México to fill in while one of the local pastors continued his studies. They did, and once again, fell in love with the people they were privileged to serve.

Then the call came to serve in Washington, D.C. as pastor of a Spanish church that was trying to decide whether it should go to an all English ministry, as attendance to the Spanish services was almost nil. They accepted that call and God blessed their ministry as it grew back into a viable Spanish congregation.

Back in Fort Ashby again, the Pinto, Maryland, Mennonite church asked my folks to serve as interim pastor, and so, hoping to be close to at least one child and grandchildren again, they accepted, but it wasn't long before a congregation in Calgary, Alberta, Canada asked if Daddy would be willing to serve as "overseer" or mentor to a couple home-grown young men whom the church wanted to see develop into their leaders.

Again, they accepted the call, but prior to their leaving my brother-in-law, Paul, who is a medical doctor, found a growth in my mother's body that turned out to be cancerous. After a struggle with the disease, the Lord used it to take her home.

He returned to Puerto Rico once more when asked by the school in Summit Hills to come and serve as spiritual counselor for the students. He loved every minute of his time there, as he renewed old friendships and was able to encourage the second and third generation of people composing the church he and others had worked to build so long ago. That one year assignment, by the way, turned into six years as he helped out in many other areas of church growth after completing his one year assignment.

Years later, reflecting on his work in Puerto Rico, he wrote, "And as for me, I am thankful that in the Lord's plans our family went to Puerto Rico and not Argentina. What I had thought to be the Lord's will for my life's work was quite different from His. As I look back to 37 ½ years of serving the Lord together with Alta in Puerto Rico, and then a bit over a year after Alta's Home-going, serving another six years on the Enchanted Isle, I can honestly say that I am satisfied. Both Alta and I gave the best years of our life there.

"Living and serving where the Lord wants you, brings the best out of you and your ministry is not in vain; souls are challenged and brought into the Kingdom which brings everlasting joy. I look forward to seeing those led into salvation through our efforts when one day the Lord says, "Come, come into my presence, my faithful son!"

There is just one more story I would like to include which points out how Daddy viewed his many "successes" as a leader and innovator in the church, especially in regards to missions. The area in central Puerto Rico called Pulguillas (a term that refers to a lively person who is not easily discouraged) is where the first Mennonite church was established, as well as the first school. I spent a majority of my growing up years at this location.

The school and mission homes are built up on the side of the hill while the church building, the largest Mennonite church in Puerto Rico, was built farther down, overlooking the road that runs through the community. There is a sidewalk that runs all the way from the top of that slope down to the church, and then on down to the road. That sidewalk is composed mainly of steps, and there are many of them.

There are a couple of rooms at the back of the church, and this is where the first recording room and studio were located. Behind the church was a small wooden building we called *"La Casita"* (the little house). The first offices of the radio broadcast Luz y Verdad were located in that building. The church and its two little rooms still stand, but the little wooden house has long since disappeared, destroyed by the voracious termites that infest the area. All that remains are the small concrete pylons that once supported the original offices of Luz y Verdad.

On a visit there many years later, Daddy and I had walked down the long set of stairs to where it had all begun, and a great sadness came over me as I saw the remnants of the beginning of what once had been a thriving ministry. After some time of silent reflection, I asked Daddy if it ever saddened him to see so much of Luz y Verdad "go up in smoke."

His reply was characteristic of how he viewed his whole ministry and service to the Lord. He said, "Sonny (he hadn't called me that since I was a small boy), all the church buildings ever built, all the programs ever broadcast, all the messages ever preached, all the correspondence lessons ever graded, all the letters ever written, all the meetings ever held, all the prayers offered up from this spot and so many others, and all the other work ever done was for the sole purpose of leading others to the Lord. They never were intended to become a monument."

For one brief moment he paused, deep in thought, as if recalling all the moments and memories of battles fought and won, and a few lost. A gentle smile came over his face, as he put his arm across my shoulders. Then he turned and slowly began the long walk back up those many steps.

Gene Hershey

9

JUSTUS HOLSINGER

Justus was born on July 8, 1911, near Harrisonburg, Virginia. He served in Civilian Public Service in La Plata, Puerto Rico, from 1943 to 1946. While there he met Salome Fast, who was serving as a nurse with Mennonite Central Committee. They were married on December 16, 1944. They returned to La Plata from 1948 to 1952, where he served as director of the La Plata Mennonite Project for the Mennonite Board of Missions and Mennonite Central Committee. After returning to the United States, Holsinger taught at Bluffton, Hesston, and Bethel colleges and was academic dean at Hesston and director of teacher education at Bethel. He served as the executive secretary of the Council of

71

Mennonite Colleges. Later he helped the Academia Menonita de Summit Hills, a K-12 school in San Juan, receive accreditation. He also wrote *Serving Rural Puerto Rico*, the definitive story of the first eight years of Mennonite mission work on the island. He passed away August 8, 2007.

———————◦◦———————

M om and Dad's love of Puerto Rico and their passion for the work of Mennonite Central Committee was evident all of their lives. Shortly after their return to the mainland U.S. in 1952, I was born. Their work in Puerto Rico had been cut short by their concern for the health of my brother, who had developed asthma. I was always disappointed that I couldn't have been born in Puerto Rico and grown up there speaking Spanish!

I loved hearing Mom and Dad tell stories about the people and work in Puerto Rico. I always looked forward to visits in our home from their Puerto Rican friends and colleagues. The camaraderie that they experienced was very evident. I was actually quite old before I learned that some of those children were not my cousins!

Since Dad wrote several histories of the Mennonite work in Puerto Rico and was the director of the project, he received much more recognition than Mom. However, Mom and Dad worked as a team. Mom had made the decision to go to Puerto Rico as a single person and was one of the first two nurses. She helped to begin the medical program in La Plata in the old wooden barracks that was turned into a little hospital. She met and married Dad there. When the babies came, her focus shifted to taking care of the family, but her efforts were still very much intertwined with Dad's.

Dad and Mom's passion for service and Mennonite Central Committee (MCC) was passed on to me. Shortly after our marriage, my husband Keaton and I went to the *campo* of Bolivia with the MCC Teachers Abroad Program (TAP). Much to our surprise (and theirs!), Mom and Dad joined us in Bolivia a year later, after Dad had retired from Bethel College. Dad became the new MCC TAP director, and again Mom worked alongside him. As a team they took on many difficult challenges! After three years in Bolivia, their passion to continue to serve led them back to Puerto Rico. They spent two years helping Academia Menonita de Summit Hills in San Juan gain full accreditation.

In 1993, my husband, three sons and I traveled with Mom and Dad to Puerto Rico. What a thrill it was for our family to see firsthand their deep love of Puerto Rico! Several times during our stay people stopped us on the street in Aibonito and La Plata with cries of "Don Justo!" "Salomé!" A man living next door to where we were staying in Aibonito recognized Dad and Mom from 50 years ago—telling us that he had been "the shoeshine boy" and had participated in the boys clubs and other activities in La Plata when Dad and Mom were living there! What a wonderful time of reminiscing with him and his wife, as they served all of us a delicious Puerto Rican meal in their home.

I am very grateful for my parents and their legacy of service with the Mennonite work in Puerto Rico.

Betty Holsinger Shenk

A nother person who was instrumental in helping me to get to know the doctrine of the Mennonites was Justus Holsinger. I just remember when he used the phrase "to cross paths," because indeed I interchange events with him on different occasions. I was his pastor in Summit Hills when working with the Academia Menonita de Summit Hills in the 1960s. But before that he was my psychology teacher at Hesston College in 1954. And then in my time in South Texas he was the coordinator for South Texas Mennonite Conference. At that time in the 1980s I was the supervisor for STMCC (South Texas Mennonite Church Council) and we used to meet at Hesston, Kansas every three months. He even suggested my name for the Associated Mennonite Biblical Seminary Board of Directors. I guess that I'll say that these people, Wilbur Nachtigall and Justus, were my main heroes that introduced me to the Anabaptist movement. And that is why I was able to serve the cause of the Anabaptist Movement in Puerto Rico through various assignments like teacher at Academia Menonita Betania, pastor of Summit Hills Church and others, counselor at the Academia Menonita at Summit Hills, coordinator of the Mennonite Voluntary Service program in the 1970s in Puerto Rico, and chaplain of the Mennonite hospitals in Aibonito and Cayey.

Ángel Luis Miranda

My parents, Justus Holsinger and Salome Fast, met in La Plata in 1944 and were married later that year. Their story can be found in *Serving Rural Puerto Rico*. Following the Civil Public Service period, they returned to Bluffton, Ohio where I was born.

They returned to La Plata in 1948 where Dad served as unit director. Mom, among her other skills, was an observant photographer with her trusty Argus camera close at hand.

In 1952, our family returned and settled in Hesston, Kansas. In those early years I recall probably several dozen Sunday evenings where we would load the family into the car and visit a Mennonite church to present the story of Puerto Rico. Dad would give an enlightening lecture while Mom operated the slide projector.

I have to think that these many presentations were key factors in building awareness and support in the Kansas area for the early Mennonite work in Puerto Rico.

I was 5 ½ when we left Puerto Rico, so my memories are fading. I now frequently question whether some of the images in my mind are from what I actually saw or whether they are from these slide shows I watched so many times.

Dave Holsinger

10

ALICE KEHL

A Canadian, Alice served in Puerto Rico for many years during the 1950s and 1960s as a missionary, as a teacher in the Mennonite Bible Institute, and as a council member of Juventud Evangélica Menonita Puertorriqueña, the Mennonite youth organization. After returning to Canada, she served in the First Mennonite Church of Kitchener Hispanic congregation.

———————◆◇◆———————

A lice Kehl was one of our Bible teachers at Academia Menonita Betania. She would always sing to our class and one of her favorites was from Ruth 1:16-17 when Ruth refused to leave her mother-in-law. *"No me pidas que te deje, porque no te dejaré. Tu pueblo será mi pueblo y tu Dios será mi Dios."* (Do not urge me to leave you or to return from following you. Your people shall be my people, and your God my God.)

Alice was passionate about following and sharing God with others. She was a hard worker and thought nothing of walking very long distances to accomplish what needed to be done. She was an example of one who gave up the comforts of this life and was willing to live simply and sacrifice for the Gospel, making the people of Puerto Rico her people for many years.

Rachel Greaser Good

11

PAUL LAUVER

Paul Lauver was born on January 12, 1923 in Carlos Casares, Argentina, son of missionaries William and Florence (Beiler) Lauver. He grew up in Argentina until the age of 15, when he returned to the U.S. to attend high school in Johnstown, Pennsylvania. He began post-secondary studies at Eastern Mennonite College, and then transferred to Goshen College, where he graduated in 1945 with a degree in theology. He later completed a master's degree in Spanish from St. Francis University, Fort Wayne, Indiana. While studying for his theology degree, he began his lifelong calling to the Christian ministry, spending many weekends serving Spanish-language churches in

Archbold, Ohio, and in Chicago. He was ordained a minister with the Mennonite Church on November 4, 1945, in Belleville, Pennsylvania.

Paul and his wife Lois M. Swihart served as the first missionaries in Puerto Rico under the Mennonite Board of Missions for 12 years from 1945 to 1957. He served as pastor of the Mennonite Church in La Plata and Rabanal. He also was a church planter starting churches in Pulguillas, Cayey and Guavate. During his years in Puerto Rico, he also was an announcer for the Luz y Verdad (Light and Truth) radio ministry, and sang in a men's quartet in the radio broadcast.

In 1957, he and Lois and their four young children returned to the US. Paul was soon called to be the pastor of the Marion Mennonite Church in Howe, Indiana, where he then served as pastor for more than 27 years from 1957 until his retirement from formal ministry in 1985. Paul died in 2013 at the age of 90.

I knew Paul and his wife, Lois, well. He was a pastor and we were in the service program.

He and Lester Hershey had both lived in Argentina and spoke Spanish fluently. I remember him as a very gentle, caring person who did lot of outreach by visiting in homes.

In some ways I also thought of him as a goodwill ambassador to the other evangelical churches of the area. (La Plata was set in between Methodist and Baptist territory of an earlier time). Paul was not as aggressive but very effective in his outreach efforts.

The only thing that I recall very vividly doing with him was when he was invited to give a lecture at a small international university (Inter American University, I think) at San Germán. He asked that a men's quartet that I was in go along and do some singing--but my memory is fading. I sang the bass part and we sang on occasion for Lester Hershey's Luz y Verdad radio program.

Paul and Lois were a good team.

Luke Birky

12

ANNA K. MASSANARI

Anna K. was born in 1926 in Fisher, Illinois, the daughter of Joseph and Elizabeth (Sommer) Massanari. She was a missionary in Puerto Rico for 32 years, arriving on the Island in 1950. Her first job was as a teacher in the Escuela Menonita Betania for the second and third grades. As part of her work, she would also drive a ¾-ton truck to the school, an hour each way, packed with students.

Anna K. was deeply involved not only in the school and its formation but in the production of music for "Luz y Verdad," the Spanish-language broadcast. She was always active in the Sunday services with the music, through teaching, and other means. Often she shared her beautiful soprano voice, blessing many individuals and enriching numerous gatherings.

In 1960, Anna K. took a job in the offices of "Luz y Verdad," correcting correspondence lessons and counseling listeners through letters. She was able to reach and touch many persons in this way. In 1977 she returned to teaching in Betania.

In 1982, she was diagnosed with malignant lymphoma and again touched many lives during those days of illness. Anna K. Massanari died in 1983.

———————

Anna K. led a class for a group of junior high girls on Wednesday nights at the Aibonito Church. One session stands out to me all these years later. She took us to her house and demonstrated how to make a cake, increasing our baking skills and building our camaraderie. This was followed by a teaching on the Heroes of the Faith from Hebrews 11. It wasn't just a Bible story, but many stories of people whose impact still reaches us today that believed in God and made a difference in their worlds.

Anna K. also believed God and left home and family to go to another land where God sent her. She gave her life to serve others by her work at Luz y Verdad, with her beautiful voice in the choir, as a teacher in the early years of Betania, in the churches she was a part of and in daily life as a friend and mentor. She was gracious and kind, a woman who trusted God and a true hero of the faith.

Rachel Greaser Good

Anna K. lived near the hospital with Mary Ellen Yoder and Carol Glick. Carol helped me learn more advanced Spanish and was an excellent teacher. Anna K. was a fellow Illinois person so we frequently shared stories about friends and relatives! She was a faithful prayer warrior and worker at Luz y Verdad, coordinating responses to mail and requests.

Roger Studer

My first teacher at Escuela Menonita Betania had the best name that I ever heard at the age of six years old, Miss Mansanari, as I pronounced it then with my Puerto Rican little kid accent.

Miss Anna K. Massanari was my teacher back in 1956-1957 in the mountains of Barrio Pulguillas near Aibonito, Puerto Rico.

She was one of the best teachers I ever had, and probably *mi favorita*, my favorite. If you ask why, it is because she was my first teacher. No kindergarten for me, since Betania didn't have one. Being the first she established the standards and expectations for a great teacher. Also, in my eyes she looked like an angel with her white hair covering. The Puerto Rican ladies of those days didn't look like that. Furthermore, she was very sweet and caring, and she had a great smile for all of us every day and every time. That means at all times!

I will never forget my first day of school for first grade at Betania. I was very excited with my new clothes, new shoes and new socks. And I was extremely nervous, knowing I was going to meet a lot of people and be away from my *mami* most of the day.

That day my mother helped me get dressed, and my oldest brother Rafael and myself rode in el *camión* to school. That was totally awesome.

The first and second grade students assembled at the school yard in front of the building where those classes were conducted. While pointing to the first grade room Miss Massanari was instructing us to form a straight line in front of it.

I remembered that I was in the middle of the line and suddenly there was a bit of commotion. A few of the students were pointing and laughing towards my way, but I was not understanding what was going on. Immediately I started to cry as I was a little girl, extremely shy and very nervous.

But that wonderful teacher right away came to my rescue. She put her arm around me and explained that the students were laughing because my socks didn't match. I was wearing different style and color socks. She told me that it was alright. That it was not a big deal and that I looked pretty for the first day of school.

Her beautiful smile put me at ease right away.

Then she said directly to me "Today is going to be a good and fun day". She was absolutely right. And afterwards every day of the school year she asked me if I was doing okay. That meant a lot to me then and now.

Having her as my first grade teacher was an absolute joy.

I will always remember my first day of school for first grade and my fantastic first grade teacher.

We were little humans those days but Miss Massanari treated us very well with a lot of love and tenderness. She had the great talent to make us interested in all the school topics, especially English, which obviously was hard for us.

She had the ability to make learning fun. Her voice was soft and at times very animated.

I really cherished those days as she gave me 'one on one' caring and loving attention.

Annabelle Falcón Trimmer

My Life Has Meaning

The day is beautiful, Lord,
As is every day we live with you.
The sun rises, the sun sets,
Moon and stars come out.
Day after day, night after night,
Season after season, Your world is ordered.
Nature follows a Divine plan.
We trust that plan for we see it has never failed.
Seedtime and harvest, you have said, year after year.
Shall our lives, then, be any less ordered?
One experience follows another in perfect sequence.
Even in seedtime and harvest, rain and clouds
Sometimes obscure the view ahead.
Clouds obscure the sun too,
But make your plan no less orderly.

So what if clouds have now obscured
The sunshine of my Betania days?
I do not see the smiling children who wait
To hear about the "letter" you have written them.
But beyond those clouds the sun still shines, I know.
And night and day continue in succession.
So shall my faith cause me to rise
Above the clouds that hide Betania from my sight
And know that order still exists
In this my life, because forever and eternally
I am yours.

Anna K. Massanari

Note: This poem was written by Anna Kay Massanari on August 18th when she had discovered that the monster of cancer was working in her body and that this had removed her from what she loved, teaching the Bible to the primary children in Betania. Her unfailing faith was an inspiration to all. She seemed to know that the time for reaping her life on earth was near. She went to be with her Lord on January 23, 1983.

María H. Rosado

13

STANLEY MILLER

Stanley was born on April 16, 1907, in Wellman, Iowa. He went to Puerto Rico in 1945 to direct the Barranquitas Baptist Academy. In 1949 he became the manager of the Ulrich Foundation Asomante Farm. He began poultry farming in 1950 and introduced artificial insemination to improve dairy herds. Later in life he grew plants and flowers and was the impetus for the Aibonito Flower Festival. He passed away on Feb. 7, 1995.

⸺◦⸺

T he work of Stanley Miller, like that of other Mennonites, has made a great social and economic impact in Puerto Rico. He arrived on the island in 1945 at a time of extreme poverty and unemployment, when serious health and malnutrition problems were causing the death of many Puerto Ricans.

He devoted his energy to creating projects that contributed to the common good and to improving the well-being of many families. He was known for his good character, his willingness to dream, his generosity, his innovative thinking, and his focus on creating new projects.

He is best remembered for his work with poultry, the industrialization of poultry farming, and the creation of the To Ricos chicken processing plant. He also worked on the industrialization of egg production, the modernization of the milking industry, and the introduction of silos for cattle feed. He was also a pioneer in flower cultivation. In addition, he served for thirty years on the board of directors of the Mennonite Hospital. In his honor, the main street leading to the Mennonite Hospital in Aibonito is called Stanley Miller.

Early Years

Stanley was born on April 16, 1907 in Wellman, Iowa, the second of eight children of Julius and Anna Miller. When Stanley was six his family moved to Vallier, Montana, where they lived a very basic existence near the Blackfoot Indians. For nearly a year they lived in tents and ate simple food. There he learned a great life lesson: you don't need great material things to be happy. The family later lived in Iowa and Florida.

The family finally settled in Elkhart, Indiana, where Stanley finished high school in 1926. To afford college he worked wherever he was given a chance. He delivered milk from 2 to 7 a.m., and worked in a shoe shop, a gas station, and a radio shop. In the summers he harvested wheat and, according to him, became an expert dishwasher. During the recession in 1929 he quit school to work as an electrician's assistant on the Michigan Central Railroad and at some point worked in the Ford factory in Detroit. He then returned to Goshen College and finished his pre-med studies, with the intention of becoming a doctor. After graduation he worked as a teacher in Harvard, New York. There he realized that agriculture was his passion and decided to enter Ohio State University, where he got a degree in Agriculture, with a major in poultry farming and livestock, with a specialization in artificial insemination, a new field at the time.

On June 25, 1936, he married Fern Lucille Miller, whom he had met at Goshen College, Goshen, Indiana. Following marriage they moved to Los Andes, New York, and later to Benton, Ohio, where Stanley worked as an agent for the Holmes County Experimental Agriculture Station and started an artificial insemination program. He focused on livestock technology and poultry farming. While there Stanley bought a dairy farm and built a house.

Arrival in Puerto Rico

His life changed dramatically when Stanford C. Yoder, a well-known figure in the Mennonite Church and president of the Mennonite Board of Mission and Charities, invited him to go to Puerto Rico and become director of the Barranquitas Baptist Academy, where in addition he would teach several classes and manage a sixty-acre agricultural project the Baptist Church had at Barranquitas. At that time a close relationship existed between Mennonites, Baptists, and Methodists and several other Mennonites also worked at the Baptist Academy, including Carol Glick, Esther Neufield, Eugene Miller, Hildegard Miller, James Hean, Mercedes Meléndez and Walter Mumaw.

In 1947, while working at Barranquitas, Stanley attended a conference sponsored by the commissioner of agriculture. The speaker, Mr. Juan Pons, the health commissioner, noted that Puerto Ricans were unhealthy and malnourished and that this was the leading cause of death among them. He underscored the urgent need to change the diet to include meat, milk and eggs. These words made such an impact on him that Stanley decided he would not return to the United States and would help improve this serious situation. In that moment he decided to devote himself to developing agricultural and poultry farming projects as a way to improve the quality of life of Puerto Ricans.

Ulrich Farm

In 1949 Stanley resigned from the Baptist Academy to become the first manager of the Asomante Farm project of the Ulrich Foundation and pursue his interest in modernizing dairy farming in Puerto Rico. The dairy farm he built featured the first automated milking parlor on the island and had a refrigerated milk tank. In 1950 he also began poultry farming on a tract he had bought in the Las Abejas sector in Asomante.

Stanley wanted to improve the quality of the livestock through artificial insemination. The Ulrich Foundation made this possible by selling semen to the island's stock raisers. The semen, sent by his stock-raising friends in Ohio, was packed in dry ice, transported to Chicago and flown to San Juan, where Western Union picked it up at the airport and took it to a private air company for transport to Asomante. The pilot threw out the package attached to a small parachute, generally over a landing strip on Stanley's farm. Stanley was thrilled to think that they were using the same semen in Puerto Rico that was being used in Ohio. As an expert in artificial insemination he derived great satisfaction from transferring this knowledge to Puerto Ricans who worked for the Ulrich Foundation. Pascual Soto and Félix Espada were the first to be trained. Stanley later recalled that this was not a profitable business, commercially speaking, but it gave continuity to the project he had started in Barranquitas and helped take the dairy industry on the island to the next level. The dairy industry in Puerto Rico has recognized Stanley Miller for his great contribution to improving the livestock of Puerto Rico through artificial insemination.

Storage Silos

During the first years of the 1950s the Department of Agriculture wanted to expand the island's dairy industry. One of its goals was to copy the feed storage system used in the United States to ensure feed availability year round, especially during times when green pastures could not be grown. Stanley, along with his friend

Johnny Hostetler and several Puerto Ricans, was asked to create a corporation under the Pastures Improvement Project to build these feed storage silos. The first silos were built along the south coast, the first one on the farm of Zacarías Rivera in Coamo. The government paid half the cost of the silos, and many were built only because of this incentive. The silos measured 20 feet wide by 60 feet high and cost between two and three thousand dollars. Between 60 and 70 of these silos were built around the island and many of them can still be found. One of them is the observation point along the road in the El Yunque Forest. When silo construction ended some members of the construction team decided to use a similar technique to build water tanks. Stanley thought the water tanks were used more than the silos.

Stanley Miller's Role in the Poultry Industry

Considering the Puerto Rican livestock improvement phase of his life completed, Stanley resigned from the Ulrich Foundation to devote himself full-time to his farm, where he had been poultry farming since 1950.

At the beginning of the 1950s Stanley Miller already stood out as a multifaceted social entrepreneur who sought through his projects to fill some of the needs of that time and who could take several aspects of agriculture and poultry farming to a high level of development. He was not the founder of poultry farming in Puerto Rico, as some might think, but he strengthened, modernized, and industrialized it and united the poultry farmers. Stanley used his entrepreneurial abilities to help with the social and economic crises of that time and to produce direct and indirect jobs that helped improve the quality of life of many Puerto Ricans.

In 1950, with the intention of getting involved in poultry farming, he bought a farm in Asomante, built a large, tall cage to protect the chickens from diseases, and bought the baby chicks. He then hired employees to care for the birds and gather the eggs because he was still working for the Ulrich Foundation. The neighbors were fascinated with what Stanley was doing and asked him for chicks. He gladly gave them to the neighbors on condition that they build a similar cage and imitate the care the hens required. These individuals later became important poultry farmers and followed him on the path he subsequently took. He knew that table egg production could be something greater than having chickens in the yard or several in a small cage. Motivated by his commitment to improve the nutrition of Puerto Ricans, he continued expanding his project and began the modern production of table eggs in Puerto Rico. By 1951 he already had 20,000 laying hens. The project had a packaging plant known as Aibonito Eggs, formed with a group of associates. The eggs were marketed under the name Huevos Aibonito. In 1952 Paul Miller, Stanley's brother, expanded the poultry farming group. He also had laying hens producing table eggs. Paul remained in Puerto Rico until 1983 and his sons Bobby Miller and Johnny Miller have continued in their father's footsteps, successfully participating in several areas of the poultry industry.

At that time a group of poultry farmers had started producing broilers. The chicken and egg production in Puerto Rico had increased, but even so 2.7 million eggs and six million pounds of chicken meat were being imported annually in 1951. There was still an important reliance on imported chicken eggs and meat. Island poultry farmers faced other problems, among them the lack of a good marketing program for local farmers, the absence of modern processing plants, and the poor condition of roadways.

Observing the demand for fresh chicken in the country in 1953 and considering all the problems in the poultry industry, Stanley saw the economic potential for the center of the island of a properly organized poultry company and, along with Johnny Hostetler and Simon Liechty, and also poultry farmers, he created Servicios Agrícolas Torrecillas. Other farmers saw what they were doing and asked to join. For them this was their only source of income. Torrecillas supported the poultry farmers and also created a link with the government to address problems.

Teodoro Moscoso, the founder of the Economic Development Company (Compañía de Fomento Económico) and Ramón Colón Torres, the secretary of agriculture, a native of Barranquitas and a friend of Stanley, supported the group's efforts. Teodoro Moscoso told Stanley that he would build a new chicken processing plant and rent it to them.

At that time, poultry farmers had small operations of about 50 chickens and would receive a commission for raising them. As the business grew some farmers had up to 1,000 birds.

In the beginning only a few poultry farmers joined the program, but in 1955 the company grew when the poultry farmers from La Plata joined. Initially, Torrecillas sold chicks, feed, and medicines. It also provided technical services to more than fifty producers in Aibonito and surrounding areas. The chicks were purchased in Pennsylvania and flown from New York to San Juan, before being transported to Aibonito. They were kept several weeks in a space below the store before being sold. Torrecillas also sold live birds to farm stores around the island that had their own processing equipment.

Puerto Rico did not have chicken processing plants, although there were market stalls where chicken were butchered. In 1954, Stanley, Johnny Hostetler and Simon Liechty built a small, simple processing plant on Stanley's farm, but Hurricane Betsy totally destroyed it in 1956. As an interesting fact, Stanley remembered that initially people did not want to buy the white, processed, packaged chicken because they thought the pale appearance indicated the bird had died because it was diseased. Little by little, however, people began to accept the product. Another thing that helped was the backing of Todos supermarkets, owned by the Rockefellers. In exchange for their support they demanded exclusive rights to the entire production, and for a time this was what happened.

Stanley began with a small financial base, which initially limited operations. Obtaining money for poultry farmers was very difficult. Stanley sought individual loans of $2,500 from the Banco de Ponce but was only approved for six farmers. His group attempted to create a cooperative, but the Department of Agriculture did not back it and it was dissolved. They later received support from the government and the Economic

Development Company to build the processing plant. The Torrecillas plant was built on two acres of land expropriated from the Serrallés family. The name was later changed to Pollos Asomante, then Torricos, and finally To Ricos. Equipping the plant and increasing distribution required capital. Local investors and investors from the United States were brought in. As we all know, in Puerto Rico it is not easy to manage the financial side of agriculture-related businesses, and even more difficult to obtain quick profits. Stanley's vision was broad and important, but the business aspect was very difficult. As with every business that starts with limited financial resources, they experienced many difficulties, but it finally began to yield profits.

Stanley also took his modern production models to neighboring Caribbean islands. The minister of agriculture of Trinidad invited him to provide guidance to poultry farmers in the neighboring islands, to help carry out a study of poultry farming there, and to offer lectures in the country. Mr. K. Murray, the president of the country's poultry farmers, coordinated the efforts.

The To Ricos chicken processing plant began operations in 1958 with modern production, management, automation, processing and marketing systems. In September of that year it began processing up to 3,000 chickens a day, and this was soon increased to 5,000. The competition came from the "yellow and flabby" imported chicken, so they began promoting the freshness of their chicken, because no one knew exactly how long the imported chicken had been frozen. To Ricos chicken cost fifteen cents more than imported chicken.

Joaquín Rodríguez notes that, as with many other large projects, not everything was a bed of roses for Stanley and his team's efforts to take poultry farming to another level. He explains that many viewed Stanley's success and vision with admiration, but a few viewed it with apprehension. They were not able to understand the potential for industrialization of poultry farming that Stanley saw. His unorthodox entrepreneurial vision initially produced some differences with government agencies and with a few of his fellow-Mennonites, who considered him "too liberal and speculative." They failed to see his vision as a social entrepreneur for a country that needed to get out of poverty and make progress. Joaquín commented that history showed that Stanley was right. Among the difficulties of converting a small enterprise into a large one, there is the challenge of meeting the incomprehension of some when one's vision exceeds the norm in a given age or situation. Sometimes it is difficult to understand visionaries.

In a conversation with his daughter Ruthie, Stanley remarked that although having undertaken this initiative caused him serious problems, he managed the challenges as best he could and came to the conclusion that everything he did it was worth the trouble. When Harry L. Frieman of the *San Juan Star* interviewed him in 1984 and expressed admiration for his work, he replied that he had only done what he had to do, that things happened because they had to.

During a business trip to New York in which he planned to meet with the Pillsbury Company to discuss business, he unfortunately suffered a serious heart attack. As a result, he was forced to cut back on his work and sell To Ricos. He wanted to sell the business to the government with the hope that it would create a cooperative under the control of poultry farmers. He offered it to Miguel Hernández Agosto, secretary of agriculture, for book value, offering also his free advice to organize it. The government thought the price was too high and in 1965 Stanley sold To Ricos to Molinos de Puerto Rico, a subsidiary of Nebraska Consolidated Mills, for a much higher price. This brought to a close Stanley Miller's participation in an important phase of the development of the poultry farming industry in Puerto Rico.

Flower Growing Industry

In 1965, to ease the strain on his heart, Stanley moved to his farm in Asomante in the Las Abejas sector, where he had built a new house. He had gradually been transforming the laying hen operation into a vegetable growing project, which he later converted into a modern plant and flower growing business covering several acres.

Freck Hart of the *San Juan Star* wrote in an article published on October 17, 1971, titled "Flowers can and do grow on Farm in Aibonito," that the colors of Stanley's flowerbeds looked like a beautiful rainbow. Stanley told the reporter of his conviction that Aibonito had almost perfect conditions for plant and flower cultivation and of his intention to stimulate and support the development of many flower growers on the island. He explained that it was not only a matter of growing plants and flowers, but of taking control, uniting, and cultivating in sufficient amount to permit export. Instead, Puerto Rico was buying millions of dollars' worth of flowers and plants. He thought that at that moment what was most needed to reach these goals was technical knowledge, long-term financing, and tax incentives for flower growers. Stanley and Tom Lockhard, another flower growing pioneer who was also a commercial-level producer, brought in experts from the United States to advise and help them with their crops. According to Stanley, there was a great need to develop specialized flower growing technicians on the island and to establish pilot programs. He explained that in building a nursery the same technologies should be applied to large and small ones. Stanley was very interested in growing long-lasting plants, observing the survival aspects and analyzing how plants adapted to the country. As part of his research he gave away plants on condition that people would take good care of them, observe them, and report on their development and adaptation after leaving the nursery.

Stanley produced many varieties of plants and cut flowers such as chrysanthemums, daisies, pom poms and anthuriums for florists and hotels. The cut flowers were cultivated at different stages and in rotating phases. The favorite of all, and the best seller, was the hybrid "White Iceberg" chrysanthemum. Around Mother's Day Aibonito Flowers could have 20,000 rose plants in production and Christmas brought an enormous production of poinsettias. Stanley inspired and supported many individuals who established their own flower growing businesses, contributing yet again to the country's economy and to job creation.

The Flower Festival

Aibonito has always been enthusiastic about flowers, perhaps because the climate is ideal for gardening. The Gardening Club, sponsored by the Agricultural Extension Service, was created in 1957. It was the third gardening club organized on the island. The members of that group were devoted gardeners and included Aida Rivera, Isabel Merly, Enelia Comas, Felícita Abad, Olga Cruz, Anita Rosario, Marshal and Malala Berard, Rafael Benítez, Fern Miller and Rafael Díaz. Joaquín Rodríguez and Jorge Luis León were the group's advisers. In 1958 the Gardening Club held the first flower, foliage, cacti, floral arrangement, and miniature garden design show in the office of Aibonito's Agricultural Extension Service. The club also participated in island-wide festivals. This participation in festivals and the enthusiasm for ornamental plants and flower growing in general generated a perfect atmosphere in which to organize a flower festival in Aibonito. Plant cultivation was on the increase and helped beautify the town. It was great therapy for gardening and flower-growing enthusiasts.

Extension agent Jorge Luis León, with the support of flower-growers Enelia Comas, Stanley Miller, Rafael Díaz, some employees of the Agricultural Extension Service, and the members of the Gardening Club organized the first flower festival in 1959. Lawrence Greaser offered the Ulrich Foundation grounds for the first events. Stanley Miller was instrumental in the planning and organization of the first festivals. Beginning in 1969 and for a few more years I had the good fortune of participating with Fern in these flower shows. In 1973 the Festival acquired ten acres of land from the Carmelite nuns. Another fifteen acres were added later. These are today the grounds of the very successful annual Aibonito Flower Festival.

Stanley's work was diverse and speaks for itself. He knew how to take an idea and develop it with passion until it became something large and innovative that produced a common good.

His work is evident when we observe how far the broiler, table egg, milk and flower industries have advanced. His projects have produced thousands of jobs. Today the island produces millions of tons of chicken meat and millions of dozens of eggs. It should be noted that his vision for modernizing and industrializing these industries produced a sustained economic prosperity in Puerto Rico. In 1990 the Puerto Rican Association of Farmers declared him "Father of the Poultry Farming Industry in Puerto Rico."

He never made a fortune for himself and Fern. His greatest treasure was his adopted family of five children, Jaime, Joe, Fernando, Ruthie and Judy; the students who received scholarships from him to pursue their academic dreams; and his contributions to the progress of the island he loved. He proclaimed that he was a Puerto Rican by adoption and from the bottom of his heart. He used to tell me that he was more Puerto Rican than I because he had lived more years on the island than I had. On one occasion he made the same remark to pro-independence leader Rubén Berríos on the plaza.

He died on February 7, 1995, when he was 87 years old, in Puerto Rico, the island that he loved.

Mary Miranda

I met the Millers for the first time in 1950 when I was a student of the Baptist Academy of Barranquitas (BAB). Wilbur Nachtigall, a personal friend of Stanley and Fern and at the time a Mennonite missionary in Palo Hincado, made the meeting possible. Together they worked the special agricultural project associated with the Baptist Academy. At this time Baptists and Mennonites worked together on education, evangelism and social assistance programs for the island of Puerto Rico, so much so that the Baptist Academy during the 1950s had a significant number of Mennonite staff.

The reason for this first meeting with Stanley and Fern concerned my economic inability to pay the tuition of the Baptist Academy. The monthly tuition for the school was around $12.00, an amount my parents could not afford. Wilbur Nachtigall informed the Millers of my family's precarious economic situation and Fern found a way to help me. She taught me to make brooches in the form of small birds. Today I am not too fond of crafts; however, as a teenager I learned to do some craft projects, including those brooches. I took the materials home and when I had finished a certain number I took them to Fern. They, in turn, sold them somewhere in the United States, the proceeds going directly to BAB tuition. This is how, thanks to them, I was able to pay for my studies. They helped many students in different ways, many of them with projects such as this. The Millers had a great mission at Baptist Academy, helping many young people of central Puerto Rico with scarce economic resources.

Over the course of time, and after various assignments with Mennonite institutions, our paths crossed again. In the 1990s, when I was serving as chaplain of the hospice program of the Mennonite Hospital in Aibonito, Stanley Miller became one of the hospice patients. In my capacity as hospice chaplain I visited him periodically. I remember that one day, during one of my first visits, Stanley was sitting in front of his house in *barrio* Algarrobos of Aibonito. I commented on the beauty of the panoramic view across the way. He answered that no matter where one is in Puerto Rico one will always have a beautiful view. He loved Puerto Rico.

During my visits I always sought to lend support, both to him with his terminal condition and to his wife. Curiously, Gonzalo Quevedo, a priest and director of the Casa Manresa, entered the hospice program the same year. They were both about the same age.

The Millers were members of the Mennonite churches in Pulguillas and Aibonito. For many years Stanley taught the English Bible class. God granted me the privilege of accompanying him in the last phase of his earthly life until time came to depart this world to meet the Lord.

Ángel Luis Miranda

O n July 4, 1960 our family moved from Coamo Arriba to

Stanley Miller's farm in the Las Abejas sector of barrio Asomante. For three generations *los Ortiz*, the descendants of Miguel Ortiz Peña, an immigrant from the Canary Island, had lived at various places of his farm in Coamo Arriba. Leaving that *barrio* surely caused my father much fear and trepidation. For my mother, María Green, it was a return closer to the Helechal *barrio* where she was born, which made the change more tolerable. Three reasons motivated the change. My brother Alfredo's vision was at risk and he was being treated by Dr. George Troyer; my father was concerned about the education of his children and in our *barrio* we could only study through sixth grade; and, learning of our family's situation, Mr. Stanley Miller offered us an empty house on his farm in Asomante. The farm grew vegetables, raised chickens, and had laying hens. Eggs were graded, packaged and sold there. All this meshed with a dream my father had in which "a large hand emerging from the top of a mountain invited him to come up." Based on this revelation my father Mariano, like the Psalmist who had faith that "even there shall thy hand lead me" (Psalm 139:10), also had faith.

Mr. Miller's intervention changed our family's life forever. It seems that the invitation to move to Stanley's farm developed when Mrs. Fern Miller heard of our family's situation from missionary families of the Betania congregation. We were a family of five brothers and three sisters. The house we were offered had three bedrooms, and although it was old we easily settled in.

The second step was to get jobs. Stanley gave my parents and brothers jobs on his farm. Initially they worked growing vegetables and at Aibonito Eggs, which my brother Rubén later managed. This move to barrio Asomante allowed my siblings to study at the Betania School in Pulguillas.

In the early 1960s I had an interesting experience that reaffirmed my admiration for Mr. Miller. Part of the Thanksgiving celebrations at Betania was an auction where all sort of things were sold. I pinned my hopes on an encyclopedia called *The Standard Bible Encyclopedia*, which had between three and five volumes. My interest was such that I ventured to make a bid for it, even with my limited budget, but others also started bidding. They were willing to offer more money and the price rose. I grudgingly stopped bidding. Mr. Mervin Nafziger paid more money and bought it. To my surprise, Mr. Nafziger later approached me, gave me the encyclopedia, and whispered to me "the encyclopedia is yours; Mr. Stanley Miller bought it for you." I used this material for a long time, thanks to Mr. Miller, the anonymous donor. That given an indication of what his heart was like.

When I returned from Goshen College in August, 1962, I rejoined the family circle. At that time Mr. Miller, whose life was then focus on poultry farming, gave our family another opportunity. A local poultry farmer had problems managing his farm and laying hen operation and had decided to abandon his small 2.5-acres farm, along with his debt. Mr. Miller cautiously approached my father and proposed that he move to the farm and care for the laying hens, but without quitting his job at the eggs plant. He suggested that my father could pay the debt with the profits from the egg production. I imagine it was not easy for an entrepreneur like Mr. Miller to do business with a farm worker who was not used to taking out loans, dealing with financial matters, or accepting the responsibility of rescuing a poultry project that had failed. After a few days of deliberation among our family, the offer was accepted and in the summer of 1963 we moved to the small farm with a little house in the Los Mangós sector.

Work on the poultry farm was a collective family project. We all worked during our free time. Years later we delivered the property deed to my father when the debt was paid off. Héctor helped with the chicken operations and Alfredo lived with my father until his final days. Thanks to the kindness of Mr. Miller we were able to move to the Las Abejas sector and later to Los Mangós. This gave our family a world of opportunities and allowed us to get ahead in life. The help we need at difficult times can appear in different forms, and that was "the hand of God" that my father saw in the dream I mentioned. We need more generous hands to undertake this type of initiative and help farm-working families on the island.

José M. Ortiz, the son of Mariano Ortiz, the one from Coamo Arriba

14

ÁNGEL LUIS MIRANDA

In Puerto Rico, Ángel Luis Miranda taught at the Escuela Menonita Betania and with the Public Department of Education. He also worked as pastor of Summit Hills, as Mennonite Voluntary Service coordinator, and as guidance counselor for the Summit Hills Academy. Ángel Luis also served as chaplain in the Cayey Mennonite Hospital. In the States he was pastor at the Alice Mennonite Church and conference administrator in Texas. He now resides in Greencroft Communities, Goshen, Indiana, with his wife Lora Eash.

W hen I think of my father, Ángel Luis Miranda, I marvel at how much ground he has covered since his birth in 1935. The first of Ramona Romero and Bernardino Miranda's eleven children, he was born in a humble two-room house in Pulguillas, a *barrio* of Coamo, Puerto Rico. My father grew up in several rural communities, most of them part of the central mountain range, with mild temperatures and thick tropical flora. Material possessions and facilities were limited. Electricity and indoor plumbing were not installed in the home until Ángel Luis was in his mid-teens. Papi recalls going to natural springs to gather water for household use, such as bathing. Papi's mother would prepare the *evento sabatino*—Saturday event—by heating water and placing it in an outdoor tub to be shared. To wash clothes, Ramonita would join the women of the community at a nearby river. Shoes were scarce, so, for a time, the kids walked and played barefoot. When they first arrived, Mennonites encountered this standard of living in the community.

The Miranda family's defining association with Mennonites began when Ramonita became one of the first patients at the La Plata Mennonite Clinic. As the story goes, the charity that Mennonites offered appealed to my grandparents. Bernardino, who had long been unsatisfied with the Catholic Church and was searching for deeper spirituality, dabbled in Rosicrucianism (Rosacruces in Spanish), a spiritual movement associated with occult philosophies. But the esoteric theories of Rosicrucianism were no match for the concrete overtures Mennonites made toward people in the community. Soon, Bernardino, aware of Wilbur and Grace Nachtigall's presence in the area, decided to attend the first Sunday worship service held in Palo Hincado, and the very next Sunday he brought the whole family with him.

Amid the Mennonite presence, some muted dissonances emerged at the intersection of culture and religion. Two Catholic priests and a nun in the area tried to discourage people from joining the Mennonite Church. Papi remembers that they admonished people, saying that every time they went to the

Mennonite church they were stomping on the cross. Yet, despite the fact that Papi and his sister Lydia were baptized into the Catholic Church as infants and were learning the catechism to prepare for confirmation, the family had never attended Mass regularly, and these admonishments did not hold much sway.

Another clash emerged even closer to home. To dissociate himself from anything remotely Catholic, Papi stopped using the traditional greeting, "*Bendición; que Dios te bendiga.*" One day, upon entering his *tía* Fela's home, he simply said "*Hola,*". Tía Fela, shocked at the utter lack of deference, started hurling insults his way. But even this familial discomfort was not enough to discourage Papi from pursuing his newfound faith. He reports that becoming Mennonite did not ultimately represent a big adjustment. Instead, he regards it fondly as his first real spiritual experience. (Side note: I lament that Papi stopped the greeting tradition. Here is how it works: when you greet your elders, you say "Blessings," and the elder responds, "May God bless you." From my distant point of view, it is nothing but lovely!)

Papi's rural Puerto Rican upbringing, surrounded by his large family and punctuated by Mennonite intervention, undoubtedly played a significant role in developing his physical and spiritual persona, characterized by frugality, adaptability, openness, and agility, and peppered with humor and silliness.

Frugality

Most Mennonite pastors, or persons associated with them, are acquainted with frugality. But being a pastor in Puerto Rico adds a complex layer to the notion of frugality; lower wages and a high cost of living force it to occupy a more primary position.

Eating out was a rare occurrence in our household. I remember going to places like McDonald's maybe twice a year, and anything fancier was virtually non-existent. One exception, no doubt influenced by Papi's strong sweet tooth, was our frequent stop on our way back from visiting Abuela in Bayamón. Mr. Donut (pronounced "Mistel Dona"), was a shop located in a strip mall on Route 2 somewhere between Bayamón and Caparra. On our stop we would delightedly devour all the different flavors in the dozen-donut box. These days Papi's sweet tooth is arguably even stronger. In my parents' pantry you are likely to discover some kind of pastry that he has snuck in, anything from sweet cornbread to pecan pinwheels, cakes and cookies. And, as much as he likes eating these things, he likes offering them to others even more. Amid the frugality Papi still finds ways to be generous. In retrospect, the stop at Mr. Donut put a smile on all our faces in a much more affordable and effective way than a full meal out.

Sometimes Papi packaged frugality as entertainment. During a summer in the late 1970s my mother, Lora, took a trip to the States to visit family. While Mami was away Papi arranged for us to spend a few days on the tiny island municipality of Culebra. He accepted an offer from an Academia Menonita de Summit Hills family to stay at their house on the island.

At the time, the US Navy controlled most of Culebra, using the surrounding waters for military exercises, thus limiting beach access. The island's infrastructure was spotty. In short, Culebra was not ideally set up for tourism.

Papi, my brother Martín, my sister Elissa and myself, set off for Culebra, first making the long drive to Fajardo and then crossing over the water on a bumpy ferry. The house where we lodged could more accurately be described as a shack with no particular charm. Our only source of drinking water (bottled water was not a thing yet) came from a rain-catching container attached to the roof. The house sat on the edge of a lagoon, and there was a paddle boat for our use.

No doubt drawing on the resourcefulness he learned growing up, Papi was able to create memorable experiences for us. For one of our meals he caught a small fish, fried it with some salt, and, grinning, presented it as a feast. Our teenage response was less than grateful.

To reach Flamenco, one of the few accessible beaches, Papi procured a *público* to take us on the three-mile trip. We hopped into the van, each of us carrying provisions consisting of simple bologna and cheese sandwiches and a few other beach-specific items. What a treat it was to arrive onto Flamenco, where only a handful of other people occupied the sands! Up to that point, even on the mainland of Puerto Rico, I had not seen such crystalline turquoise waters. Even better, no buildings spoiled the palm-filled scenery. All this courtesy of my father! But then, after a half-day at the beach, as if to teach us a life lesson, Papi announced we would be walking back. Grumble!

Papi's manifestations of frugality taught me the value of simplicity, which can be frustrating on the surface, but rewarding if surrendered to. That is, having the best and most, materially speaking, does not always translate to having the best experience. At one time our misguided teenage minds blinded us to what was worthwhile, but, little by little Papi guided us toward the overlooked riches readily available to all of us.

Adaptability

My father began flexing his adaptability muscle early in his life with family moves within Puerto Rico. In mid-20th century Puerto Rico, many families moved around hoping to find better job opportunities. The Miranda Romeros were no exception. At one point Bernardino worked as a traveling salesman, offering wares such as shoes—a near luxury at the time—and a rub called Emulsión Jiménez. Intent on maximizing his sales and in search of better housing, Bernardino led the family to live in Salinas, Aibonito, Coamo, Asomante, Palo Hincado and, once my father was in college, an area of Bayamón known as Los Millones. But Bernardino's search for better employment went even further, culminating in steel mill work in Lorraine, Ohio, and Gary, Indiana, where he would stay for an extended period during a given year before returning home to Puerto Rico.

Nowadays in the United States we sometimes worry about the negative effects that moving may have on children and adolescents. Yet, we forget that much good can come from the experience of living in multiple places. Such was the case with Papi, who believes that in light of a simple upbringing his exposure to so many places opened up his mind. Indeed, this early nomadic experience in Puerto Rico set the tone for future challenges. By the time he set off for college he was sufficiently equipped to deal with the cultural differences he would face in the U.S., which were more pronounced than they are today.

Papi's experience adapting came in handy during his time at Hesston College. Despite having to contend with much colder temperatures and gloomier days than he had ever experienced in Puerto Rico, Papi's time at Hesston and Goshen Colleges was mostly positive. It was a time for him to deepen his understanding of the Mennonite faith tradition and to hone his calling to pastorship through study and relationships.

Justus Holsinger, Papi's psychology professor at Hesston, was one such relationship that endured. Papi was already acquainted with Justus, since he was second only to Wilbur Nachtigall arriving in Puerto Rico as a Mennonite. Much later, during his tenure as pastor in Alice, Texas, Papi would again cross paths with Justus. The two would often see each other at South Central Conference events, and this led to Justus recommending that Papi be on the Associated Mennonite Biblical Seminary Board.

Another relationship with Hesston roots was that of a woman he admired from a bit of a distance, as she sang in a treble quartet. The warbling woman went on to graduate from Goshen College with a degree in education, taught for a year in Kalamazoo, Michigan, and found her way to Puerto Rico, having accepted a two-year voluntary service term on the island. Lora Esch cut her term short, however, to marry Ángel Luis.

Whereas Papi would never characterize Mennonites as having a negative influence on him personally, or on Puerto Ricans in general, as he gained more exposure to Mennonites in the U.S. he confronted some disheartening and problematic issues, mostly having to do with race and culture. After all, he was entering a space of predominantly white people of German extraction. At best, these people could at times be culturally insensitive, even in academia.

After grading an exceptionally well-written paper my father wrote, a Hesston professor asked, "Is this your work?" as if he could not have possibly written it on his own. By the time Papi arrived in the United States, his English proficiency was advanced. However, he struggled speaking the language, not because he did not understand it but because he was literally tongue-tied. His frenulum was attached to his mouth. Imagine trying to speak a second language with a physical impediment in your tongue. This could only have intensified any lack of intelligibility from an accent, and it caused my father some insecurity. Still, it would not have required much from this professor to think more broadly about the situation. Instead, Papi was met with the hurtful language we might call a microaggression these days. Papi did not have the benefit of naming it thus, and he dealt with the hurt feelings privately. Happily, Papi's tongue was eventually surgically untied during the time he spent working at Billjax in Archbold, Ohio. His boss noticed Papi's speech troubles, and upon learning the reason behind it he covered the cost of the surgery.

Papi had to contend with other cultural insensitivities, such as racist white Mennonite parents who did not want their daughter to date her Puerto Rican friend, simply because he was Puerto Rican. But the insensitivity was not limited to individual interactions. For a time the Mennonite Church discouraged missionaries from engaging in romantic relationships with people they encountered in Latin America. Thankfully, my parents were either blissfully unaware of this misguided directive or they chose to ignore it. Otherwise, I might not be writing this!

What is Papi's conclusion about these insensitivities? He says, "I take the cultural differences as an opportunity to better myself. I try to see people at their core." These words offer a glimpse into my father's interpretation of Christian life, the kind of Christian life of which he saw an example in the Mennonites that first arrived in his community, centered in charity, both material and spiritual.

Openness

My father's social approach has always been outward looking. By my observation, he lacks some of the hangups many of the rest of us have talking to strangers. He is genuinely interested and curious about people, even when there are barriers to connecting.

When my parents came to visit me at the end of my junior year of college in Strasbourg, France, I met them at Orly airport in Paris, and, immediately, we hopped on a Brussels bound train to spend some time with our cousins Betsy and Bruce McCrae and their children, who were living there at the time. We found seats next to a young woman traveling alone. Naturally, my parents were physically tired after their eight-hour trip, but they were both palpably excited to be in Europe. As the train crossed the Northern French fields, Mom, between nodding off, said with a huge smile, "Look at the cows!" I responded, "You have seen cows before," to which she responded, "Yes, but these are French cows!" Papi, on the other hand, was directing his attention to the woman next to us and started speaking to her in English. He asked, "Hello, where are you from?" My first thought was that we were in France and he could not assume that people spoke English. That did not stop him, though, and, indeed, this woman answered in very few words. But even though no robust verbal exchange ensued, Papi succeeded in making a human connection, which is more than would have happened in his absence. As a result, smiles abounded!

Agility

Papi has always tended to be physically active. I have memories of my father playing baseball, sprinting, and most of all, playing ping pong. At Summit Hills we often kept a ping pong table in the *marquesina*, and we kids would take turns playing matches with Papi, and losing 99 percent of the time. The Summit Hills Mennonite Church sometimes sponsored ping pong tournaments held at Academia Menonita, and often Papi and Daniel Schipani were the finalists.

Ping pong and other physical outlets represented a counterbalance to Papi's otherwise serious work as a pastor and servant of the church. His inner child definitely comes alive when he is playing a match. He chuckles, strategizes, slides from side to side, and, yes, gets rather competitive. Even now, at Greencroft, Papi participates in near-weekly ping pong matches, which has kept him a young octogenarian.

Humor

Inevitably, laughter has always made its way through Papi's large and boisterous family. Each of my father's siblings holds varying proportions and qualities of humor. Jorge is the master of ceremonies humorist, often holding court during family reunions and using his dry delivery like a stand-up comedian. Haydeé, ever the talker, tells stories of quirky events and comes up with witty assessments of them. Enrique is funny without even knowing it. And then there is Ángel Luis's brand of humor: word play.

Papi likes to connect words by drawing out similarities in spelling and pronunciation. Among other things, he has analyzed all of Puerto Rico's municipalities and discovered patterns. For example, the three-letter cluster *gua* appears in Caguas, Naguabo, Guayama, Guaynabo (I may have missed some!). Or, he'll wonder out loud if the founders of Nappanee, Indiana, had the habit of sleeping while kneeling—nap on knee. The area in Puerto Rico called Guavate, known for its pig roasting (*lechón*), to Papi is a place where the *lechón* is consumed with guava, as in "guava ate."

He has been known to make up words for situations without adequate descriptors. One such word is *mafarunga*, which refers to waking up feeling tired and experiencing a physical malaise that has no explanation. One might say, "Could you make me some coffee, please, to see if my *mafarunga* goes away?"

Sometimes he'll use existing words to rethink events, such as his daily "invitation." Papi gets "invited" to his after-lunch nap every single day. It must be nice to be so wanted! Another such term: "relaxing coffee." There's coffee along with breakfast, and then there's coffee sometime after breakfast—relaxing coffee.

Calling these things humor might be a stretch, but they often lead to utterances that elicit a sort of half smile from whoever happens to be around, like the reaction to a Dad joke.

My father has experienced pivotal moments that have required him to reconcile conflicting forces and make difficult decisions because of the unknowable. My father has surrendered to these moments, trusting that his faith will lead him through.

In the late 1960s, sponsored by the Mennonite Church, my parents were slated to move to Brussels, Belgium, to work with the Spanish speaking immigrant population. But, at a relatively late stage in planning, another candidate expressed interest in going. Whereas my parents were in metropolitan San Juan, the other candidate was a rural Mennonite. At the time, the Puerto Rico Mennonite Convention was comprised of a majority rural representation. In order to decide who would go to Brussels, the Convention held a vote, and the other party was elected. My father was certainly disappointed, but soon another opportunity emerged, that of seminary studies in Montevideo, Uruguay. It is thus that, as a family, we experienced two of the most memorable years of our lives.

Much later in his life my father (and mother) had to pivot again when plans for a pastorship in Indiana fell through. After a short time in Goshen my parents moved back to Puerto Rico, where my father eventually found employment as chaplain of the Mennonite Hospital in Cayey. In the end, my father's naturally caring and social manner harmonized with the ministry at the hospital. This venture even earned him attention from the *San Juan Star*. Identifying him as one of Puerto Rico's hidden heroes, the newspaper published an article featuring his service at the hospital. In retirement Papi continues to volunteer his time providing companionship to ailing immigrants at the Center for Healing and Hope in Goshen.

Exploring Ángel Luis's characteristics and experiences has exposed recurring themes of selflessness, kindness and love. I can only conclude that my father's faith, first planted by his encounter with Mennonites, has led and continues to lead his approach to life. One could say that he is not so blessed to have found Mennonites, so much as Mennonites are blessed to have found him.

Eric Miranda

15

WILBUR NACHTIGALL

Wilbur Nachtigall was born on November 17, 1918, in Hamilton County, Nebraska, and died on October 2, 2003, in Iowa City, Iowa.

He was the first director of the La Plata Project, from June 24, 1943 to July 24, 1945. He married Grace Kauffman, who had been a nurse in La Plata, in 1946. Wilbur was ordained in Iowa in 1948. Wilbur and Grace returned to Puerto Rico in 1949 and served in evangelical and medical work until 1955.

After returning to the States, Wilbur served as pastor of several churches. He obtained his M.A. and Ph.D. in Spanish and taught at the University of Iowa and Illinois Wesleyan University. In

January 2003, Wilbur and Grace were honored by the Puerto Rican community by having a chapel in the new Mennonite Hospital in Cayey, Puerto Rico, named after the founders.

———◦———

I have good memories of the Wilbur Nachtigall family. It was through Wilbur Nachtigall that I first learned about the Mennonite Church. They were the first missionaries to come to Palo Hincado in Barranquitas, P.R. He was instrumental in helping the young people get their high school education through making rugs. And in my case he helped me to come to the U.S. in 1953 so I could attend Hesston and Goshen Colleges. He really had the gift of working with us young people.

Ángel Luis Miranda

On the Wings of a Hurricane (from Wilbur Nachtigall's Autobiography)

The date was September 19, 1949. A Puerto Rican day-laborer brought his wife to Mennonite General Hospital in La Plata. According to the birth certificate, this was her seventh child. She was 25 years old. One might say that the little baby girl arrived "on the wings of a hurricane." September is the month that spawns more hurricanes in the Caribbean than any other month. With a hurricane storming across the Leeward Islands, all patients were moved from the flimsy frame barracks building to the more substantial concrete building, the community center. Nurses told us later that the newly born child did not take the move very well. She suffered from colic. She cried almost constantly.

We were in the midst of a move ourselves. When the hurricane struck, we were still occupying the pastor's house, adjacent to the church in La Plata. During the hurricane, some dozen or so unit members came to our house to spend the night. The parsonage was constructed of concrete and offered needed protection. When the storm subsided, we carried out the mission plan and moved to

111

our new out-post at Palo Hincado near Barranquitas.

In the meantime, on September 28 the father of the new baby appeared at the hospital to call for the mother and child. It was the ninth day after the birth. While he was at the hospital desk, arranging for the discharge of mother and child, he was summoned to the bedside of his wife. She was dead of an embolism. Deeply saddened, he climbed the steep paths that led to the tiny one-room shack on the crest of the mountain ridge far above La Plata. It became his duty to inform the six children that their mother would not be returning.

As a day-laborer, he worked with hoe and pick in the tobacco fields for one dollar a day. And that only when there was work, since agriculture provided only seasonal employment. In the home the duties of the mother now fell to the oldest child, an eleven year old, scarcely prepared for such responsibilities. The new baby remained in the hospital, unclaimed for the time being. The narrative now has to be interrupted in order to explain how we fit into it.

As told earlier, we had just moved to a rural barrio about a 45-minute drive from La Plata. The cement block building that we were trying to convert into a home-church facility lacked modern conveniences. The large square room was divided into two parts by cloth screens down the center. There was open space both at the bottom and the top of the screens. On one side of the screens we made our home. There was no plumbing. A home-made wash stand with a water bucket, some home-made shelves, a refrigerator and kitchen stove made up the kitchen. Next to it was the dining room with a table I had built. We bought four chairs. Beyond these was a sofa-bed that I built, and our beds and a chest of drawers, also home-made. There were no partitions. The furniture identified the "rooms." In the rear there was a door that led into another area. It housed the bakery oven. It had become a breeding place for varmints. We needed to keep this door tightly closed so that we would not be surprised by rats in our living area. Out of the back door of this area there was a path that led up a steep incline. There sat the latrine. When it rained the path became treacherously slippery. It rained often.

In the main part of the building, on the other side of the flimsy screens, was our meeting place. Plain, backless benches, built by a carpenter at the mission, were set in rows facing the little platform at one end. A homemade pulpit stood on the platform. From that pulpit I preached my first Spanish sermons. There I taught Sunday school with a small group who helped me stumble through my first lessons taught in a new language that I was trying to learn. They were very patient. At first, it was a mother and four little children. Then, a few others stopped by, curiously wondering what was happening. Even before we moved to the "bakery" in Palo Hincado, we were making afternoon trips to La Cuchilla, trying to revive a dormant Baptist work in a termite-riddled frame chapel. Sunday afternoons, about the time we would make our visits to La Cuchilla, it would rain hard. The last mile, which had to be walked, would turn into a quagmire of red clay mud. Our Sunday schedule was demanding: between Palo Hincado and La Cuchilla I preached three times, and both Grace and I taught Sunday school twice. Then, it was decided we needed help. Of course, between leading the hymns and preaching and teaching, we needed to go out every day on visitation. We were left little choice: either we spent much of the week in preparation for Sunday—and no one came to the services; or we spent the week in the hills with the people, where we brought medical aid, became acquainted with our neighbors, and ministered to many needs—and the attendance continued to grow. Of course, there was no doubt about our choice. After all, what was the need for all this preparation if no one would show up on Sunday morning, afternoon, and evening? There was no ready-made congregation awaiting us with open arms. The congregation had to be built. When the mission sent us Sunday help, Grace responded by adding a Sunday rice and bean dinner for some nine to twelve people.

It was exciting. By October it was to become even more exciting. Here's how.

In early October we were in La Plata on business. Two nurses who conducted a Sunday school and medical clinic in Rabanal, in the mountains high above La Plata, told us about the little motherless baby from their area. The father had not called at the hospital to take the child home. They surprised us, saying, "You folks don't have children. Why don't you ask the father if he will give you the child?" The idea stopped us short. Why not? As it turned out, there was a need for quick action. There was no time for long deliberations, ponderous consultations with various and sundry mission committees, and a nine-month pregnancy. October 11 found us at Rabanal to visit Manuel León, the father of the child. He listened. Then he said, "I have already given the child away. We can't take care of her in our home. The hospital had told us that we have to get her. So, I have made arrangements with two old ladies to take her and raise her. They take orphan children." We were not easily daunted. "Could we go and talk to them?" I asked. Well, yes, he supposed we could; but he did not intend to go back on his word if they insisted upon receiving the child. So Manuel León and I started our long trek down the mountainside.

It was not a short distance. It must have been at least a 45-minute hike over difficult mountain paths. Grace remained at the house. I hiked. Down, down, down! We arrived at a secluded spot where two elderly women were washing clothes in the brook. They looked up. Before either of us could say a word, one of them said, "I know what the *americano* wants. He wants the little baby." After some gentle persuasion, they both consented, adding that *los americanos* could probably give the child advantages that they were unable to provide. Back up the mountain we climbed. Up, up, up! Are these "labor pains" I wondered?

Back at the house, Grace and I agreed there was no time to lose. It was a long return trip via paved road to the hospital. The sun was still high in the sky. Having arrived at the hospital, we announced our mission. Nurses prepared a layette, such as was given poverty-stricken people when they took their new-born home. We had made no preparation for the arrival of a child. No elaborate nursery. Not even a cradle for our new baby. She was twenty-one days old, very tiny, with beautiful brown eyes. How curious! When I was a child I had always wanted brown eyes, and I would have traded my blonde curls any day for straight, black hair!

We returned to Rabanal so that the two nurses, Marjorie Schantz and Linda Reimer, could meet our new baby. She managed to soil my trousers when we gave her the bottle before finally leaving for home. It was a "badge" that I wore most proudly.

It was after midnight when we finally arrived at our camping-style home in Palo Hincado. It had been a long, but very eventful, day. We still had to improvise a crib for our new baby. A pasteboard box, which had contained our radio-wire recorder, was pressed into service. A pillow fit just right and served as a mattress. We looked at each other and said, "We have the beginning of a family that we have always wanted." We named her Barbara Helen, agreeing that we would call her Elenita, the Spanish version of Helen. As we soon discovered, Elenita became Nita, the name she has used ever since.

During the ensuing days, many of our neighbors came to see her. Even more did not ask to enter. They merely stood at the windows and looked in, i.e., they stood at the window openings that had heavy wooden shutters. Any number commented: *"Es de nosotros"*. ("She is one of us.")

Try as we might, we could not shake the fact that there were five other children up there in that one room shack, perched so precariously on top of the mountain ridge. An eleven-year-old named Mary was caring for them. The house had no kitchen. An earthen *fogón* on which meals were prepared was attached to a rear door. It was shielded from the weather by a lean-to. The oldest son, Manuel, had to fetch water in a five gallon tin container carried on his head. It was a long way down and a long climb back up the steep path. In the single room there was a three-quarter bed. The youngest child, Lidia Rosa, slept on a goatskin. The rest slept on hammocks strung about at night. The only furniture was a little bench. On one wall there was a little shrine with pictures and candles to the Virgin Mary. Here any one of the children who might "transgress" had to kneel and pray penitential prayers. A trunk in which family "valuables" were stored stood in one corner. Yes, there was another small room on the end of the house opposite the "kitchen." It could not be entered from inside the house, but had its own door to the outside. It was kept locked. It served as a storage room for home-distilled rum, which Manuel made and sold for added income.

Our two nurses, who served as liaisons between the family and us, sent word that the load for the oldest child was becoming too burdensome. On a visit the nurses discovered that neighbors had stopped at the home. When they found the child distraught, they decided that rum would solve the problem. It had caused her to become hysterical. The two-year-old had attached herself to her older sister when her mother did not return. Mary carried her around on her hip constantly. Otherwise the child cried incessantly. "Wouldn't it be better to ask the father if the two-year-old might join her sister in your home?" the two nurses suggested.

In response to this suggestion I made another visit to the home. I pointed out to the father the advantages of keeping the two youngest children together. He agreed that it was only a matter of time before he would have to parcel out the younger children to relatives. Very likely! However, his concern was that the little Lidia Rosa, who was his pride and joy, would not adapt to our home. Finally, he agreed that it was worth a trial. He insisted that Mary would have to come with her and stay a week in order to see if the transition could be made smoothly. Linda Reimer and Marjorie Schantz arrived. Manuel (or, Papi, as he was known in the family) accompanied the two "midwives." I thought, and Grace agreed: "That little two-year-old is a most beautiful child." When I first saw her in the home she had a bad cold. There she sat, very runny nose and all, in the middle of the only bed. Her lovely red hair was twisted in brown paper strips to enhance her long curls.

After Papi departed it was obvious that she would have as few dealings with us as possible. All of her attention was focused upon Mary, her oldest sister. It became clear that she, as well as Mary, were not accustomed to eating at a table. She kept her gaze fixed upon the cement floor, refusing to look up at us. Her sister continued to carry her on her hip. When there were temper tantrums—and there were!—she looked to her sister for remedy. We, of course, could not touch her. To have done so would have provoked a torrent of protest, which, in turn, would have been interpreted by her sister as a sign that she could not become accustomed to us. Any intervention on our part would have terminated any hopes for her coming to live with us.

The weekend approached. I had a preaching appointment at another church which was located about halfway between Palo Hincado and Rabanal. I would meet our two nurses there, and Mary could return to her home with them. Mary, with a maturity beyond her years, agreed that it was a good plan. Yet, it was obvious how painful the parting would be. Lidia Rosa would go to sleep. Then Mary would leave with me.

It was a poignant, yet necessary moment, when Mary bid farewell to her little sister, sleeping peacefully in her bed. But it had to be. What maturity and poise Mary demonstrated, as she took leave of the child that had been the pride and joy of the home, especially when their mother did not return from the hospital.

Grace relates that when Lidia Rosa awoke from her nap, she immediately asked for Mary. On her own, she initiated a search of the premises. Her search took her to every part of the building, including the area where we conducted worship services. Finally, she returned to Grace, saying, *"Caramba, ¿dónde esta?"* ("For pity sakes, where is she?") Grace explained that Mary had to leave. She added, "Now I am your Mommy." There was no protest; complete acceptance seemed to be her response. She played for a while. Then she indicated that she was sleepy. Before the evening was over she addressed Grace as *"Mami."* Grace placed her in her bed. First, standing in her crib, she waited. Then, fatigue taking over, she sank to her knees. Finally she lay down and went to sleep without a whimper.

On a subsequent visit to Rabanal, Manuel noted that the two children seemed to have made an adjustment to our home. He confided that he had a problem with his son, eleven-year-old Ángel Manuel. The boy was not in school. In order to attend classes he had to walk a long distance. Further, he had to cross a river with no bridge. When the river was swollen, he did not attend at all. He felt the boy was being influenced by bad companions in the area. Then, a surprise: "Will you take Ángel Manuel and rear him in your home?"

On August 14, 1951, he arrived. All he brought with him were the clothes on his back. He wore borrowed shoes. When Christmas approached, I felt it would be a treat for Ángel Manuel to make a trip to San Juan with us. He had never been far from his rural home. He agreed. En route we stopped at a service station. Taking him to the restroom, I pointed to the toilet, asking whether he needed to use it. Earnestly looking up at me, he asked: *"¿Pa' que?"* ("What for?") Julio, who lived with us at the time, gave him his first bath at our house; and otherwise, he helped the child become acclimated to us and our home. He readily accepted the two little girls as his sisters. On previous visits to the Rabanal home I noticed a little, blue-eyed youngster, about five, who stood timidly in the corner. I learned that Ramón— for that was his name—had been given to Papi's sister to rear. When I inquired, I was told that he was Tía María's little errand boy. She kept him at home to gather firewood, sweep the patio, and do many other errands, while her own son, Cristóbal, was in school. (Ramón told me later: "If I ever see that Cristóbal again, I'll punch him in the nose!" It has been noted that Ramón has a "forgiving spirit," because many years later when his first son was born, he named him "Christopher," i.e., Cristóbal!)

I pointed out to Papi that María's decision to keep Ramón at home while she sent her own son to school did not make sense. He recognized the inequity of María's arrangement.

Sometime later we visited in the home of María's neighbors, the Juan Colón family. Ramón came over, dressed in his very best clothes and his hair neatly combed. He was still his bashful self. We learned later that he had confided in his friends that if the *americanos* invited him to live at their house, he would jump at the chance to go. When he arrived for a visit, it was almost a "done deal." Yes, Ramón could join Ángel Manuel, Lidia Rosa, and Nita at our house.

Ramón confided in his brother, "If I ever get there I won't ever leave!" And he didn't. Grace noted that Ramón seemed to be slightly crippled. The condition, however, was quickly remedied. He did not own a pair of shoes. His borrowed shoes were much too small! In fact, when he removed them, his feet were blue. It was a situation with a simple cure. He treasured his new shoes and took very good care of them.

It was now February 1952. In March 1948, we had mourned the death of a son. We had been advised that the option of adoption held little hope for us. We were "too rootless." Now we had four children. They were not adopted as yet. That was to happen later. It would be a long and tedious process.

We had to review their names given the possibility that they would live in an English-speaking environment sooner or later. Ángel is a common name in the Hispanic culture. It translates about as well as Jesús into an English culture. So we said, "Let's call him Johnny." He has been know ever since as John Manuel. Ramón translates well. When years later he was officially adopted at the age 26, he was officially named Ramón León. The family surname is León. Since carrying on the family name is very important to Papi, we preserved it in Ramón's name. Years later he seems to have anglicized it to Ray. Today it seems that we are the only ones who call him Ramón. We think it is a fine name; however, we also appreciate Ray. Lidia Rosa presented a further choice. Lidia is a beautiful Spanish name. We realized, however, that Lidia would translate to Lydia; and she would become "Lid the Kid." So, we decided on Rosa María or Rose Mary. Rosa it has remained. Today she has a granddaughter who is Karina Rose. We were not aware that Papi had named our youngest until her birth certificate arrived in the mail. He had named her Luz María, which translates Light Mary. So she kept the name we had given her on the day she came to live with us, namely, Barbara Helen. She promptly became Elenita, which resulted in the name she has used ever since, Nita. There was the time we moved from Colorado to Iowa in 1959 that she decided that she would now be known as Barbara. But that lasted for only a few days. All this confusion of names has been somewhat of a trial at times. Only recently Nita's purse was stolen, and she was deprived of all her identification. Sometimes it becomes a trial to prove one's own identity!

The adoption procedure for the girls was begun immediately. Papi declared he did not oppose the legal adoption of the two girls. He was not prepared to consent to the adoption of the boys. He asked that we rear them; but he wanted the family name preserved. We agreed, initiating the adoption of the girls at once and deciding that the boys should make their own decision regarding adoption.

We still needed to deal with the Mennonite Board of Missions. E. C. Bender, treasurer of the board, was in Puerto Rico on an administrative mission. He came to Palo Hincado. The two girls promptly won his heart. He had a wonderful time with them. The adoptions were promptly approved by the Board. Later E. C. Bender's son John, a handicapped youth, assumed the financial support of Nita. When we visited their home in Pennsylvania, he gave the children a tour of the farm, introducing them to all the farm animals. It became a fond memory for all of us, especially when John Bender died some years later. Rosa's support was assumed by the Red Top Mennonite congregation near Bloomfield, Montana. We thought it appropriate that Rosa with her red curls should be beneficiary of the Red Top congregation. John's congregation was Petosky, Michigan; Ramón's, Middlebury, Indiana.

The adoption of the girls was in process three years. The social worker who handled the negotiations with Papi and family was fortunately a very good friend, Lidia Ester Santiago. There was no manipulation on our part. It seems to have been "an act of God."

Usually there is a strong attempt to avoid a "change of religion" in the process. She told us there was not a single member of the León family who brought up the fact that this adoption would result in such a change. She found cordial support for the adoption among all family members. Yet, the fact that the adoption moved so slowly was a concern. At any time in those three years Papi could have appeared on our doorstep and demanded the return of the children. I used to have nightmares about it. To have given up the children after three years would have been devastating. Yet, our day in court finally arrived. The judge in whose courtroom the hearing took place was most cordial and helpful. When I was called to the witness stand, Nita now age 3, wandered happily about the courtroom, singing a hymn that we sang frequently in our church services. Its title line is *"Busca Dios,"* i. e., "Seek God while there is yet time." The judge was amused. It was a happy day when the final papers arrived.

As indicated, the adoption decision was left with the boys. From time to time we were made aware they talked about it. Johnny was hesitant. Ramón, in the Hispanic tradition, respected the judgment of his older brother. Then, when he was to marry Marilyn, he asked if it might be possible to have a legal change of his name to Nachtigall. He added, "But it would be better if you could adopt me." We promptly began legal proceedings. Papi was living in New Brunswick, New Jersey, at the time. All of the papers had to be prepared in Spanish and English. We travelled to New Jersey, where we were faced with the task of explaining what this adoption would mean to Papi. He was living with his daughter, Ana Hilda. He agreed to all of the adoption provisions. When it came time for him to appear at the courthouse, he firmly announced that he no longer would leave the house. It seemed we had reached an impasse. If it had not been for Ana Hilda, I doubt that we could have persuaded him to make his court appearance. She said that this adoption is good; that it must happen; and that she was taking events into her own hand. She loaded Papi almost bodily into her car, and it was full-speed ahead to the courthouse. We discovered that it is difficult to adopt babies; but it is even

121

more difficult to adopt a 26-year-old!

With John an adoption remained moot. We did not coerce. He has not been legally adopted. He has not asked for a legal change of name. We leave it at that.

From Wilbur Nachtigall's Autobiography

16

ADDONA NISSLEY

Addona was born to Amish parents on July 8, 1924, at Exeland, Wisconsin. He went to Puerto Rico in 1948, where he worked in the La Plata hospital laundry. In 1950 he returned to the United States, where he enrolled at Eastern Mennonite College. He married Mary Stauffer in 1953. Later that year a bout of back pain kept him in bed for six months, so that he wasn't able to graduate. In 1955, having recovered, he returned to Puerto Rico as pastor of the La Plata Mennonite Church. While on furlough from 1961-63, he completed college and took seminary courses. In 1963 he returned to Puerto Rico as pastor of the Mennonite church in Coamo, where he served until 1971. After returning to the States he taught Bible and Spanish, served in church administration, and as interim pastor in several congregations. He passed away on August 23, 2014, in Harrisonburg, Virginia.

———◦———

A ddona was a man of deep faith. As a young Amish man he gave his life to Christ, kneeling in prayer behind the barn. Later, unhappy with how his life was going, he prayed again, asking God to "Do whatever it takes" for him to be totally committed.

A few weeks later, Addona, who was engaged, was on a lake in a rowboat with his fiancée and another young Amish couple. The rowboat tipped over. When Addona surfaced, he saw that she was missing. He dove and found her. He grabbed her and tried to bring her up, but confused, she struggled. He finally had to come up for air, then went back down, but couldn't find her. She died in that tragic accident.

Although farming was going well, he felt led to service. He applied to Mennonite Central Committee, expecting to serve in Europe, but instead was accepted for service in Puerto Rico. In 1948 he went to La Plata, where he worked in the hospital laundry.

When Addona went to Puerto Rico in service as a single man, it was a cultural revelation. As a member of the Amish he had felt looked down on by the non-Amish culture. In Puerto Rico he felt accepted, and soon made friendships with local Puerto Rican young people.

He quickly learned Spanish and began teaching Sunday school. Paul Lauver advised him to return to the States, get his college degree, and then return to Puerto Rico as a missionary.

In 1950, Addona's service term ended. He returned to the States, took his GED and enrolled at Eastern Mennonite College. He married Mary Stauffer in 1953. That fall he developed severe back pain and spent six months in bed. After recovering he taught Spanish at Lancaster Mennonite High School and worked with Puerto Rican migrant farm workers during the summers.

In 1955 he was asked to return to Puerto Rico for missionary service. There he served as pastor in La Plata, Rabanal and Honduras. From 1961-1963 he was on furlough in Goshen, Indiana, where he finished college and took seminary classes.

In 1963 he was invited to return to Puerto Rico as pastor of the Coamo congregation. Enrique Ortiz, co-pastor with Addona at Coamo, tells how Addona was very outgoing and greeted people with a vigorous handshake. People knew that his *saludo era de corazón*. He got to know many people in Coamo, became friends with some of the Catholic priests in town, and was invited to preach in one of the Catholic churches. His sermon was well received, punctuated by calls of *Amén* from the congregation.

He had deep connections to the Puerto Rican people. Many times after church he would visit with church members, sharing a laugh, giving counsel, or sympathizing with them. He was loved by people in Puerto Rico.

Addona was very sensitive to others. Enrique recounts that when friends in the U.S. sent Addona money to buy a car he consulted with Enrique to see how this would be perceived and was assured that as a pastor who traveled a lot, people would understand his need for reliable transportation. He bought a VW bug, one of the least expensive cars available.

While in Coamo, Addona was instrumental in building a new church with a striking design.

Addona often spoke at youth retreats, using his own story of dedicating his life to Christ, asking God to "Do whatever it takes," then losing his fiancée, to invite young people to accept Christ into their lives.

Addona always wanted to do his best. This meant taking on a heavy workload. As pastor, he preached Sunday morning and also in the Sunday evening and Wednesday evening services. Then he would go into the community for Tuesday and Thursday evening visitation.

On top of this he took on the role of Executive Secretary of the Puerto Rico Mennonite Church Convention. This meant working two days a week in Aibonito. At one point the strains of the job became too much and he began experience fainting spells. The doctor told him "Even God had a day of rest," and prescribed one day a week of rest. Mark remembers the family often having picnics on Monday, Addona's day off.

When the family returned to the States in 1971, Addona was able to use the skills he had acquired in Puerto Rico, first teaching Bible and Spanish, later by being involved in church administration and then in a series of interim pastorates. Addona's life was one of submission to God's will and purposes, humility, and a deep love of people.

Tom Lehman, from interviews with Mark Nissley,
Fidel, Patricia and Rolando Santiago, Enrique Ortiz, and Addona's
autobiography

17

ENRIQUE ORTIZ

Enrique Ortiz worked as a mechanic at Ulrich Foundation and served in I-W at the Casa de Salud in Aibonito. Later, he worked in maintenance in government housing and at the Academia Menonita Betania. He served as pastor in the Aibonito and Summit Hills Mennonite churches and as Executive Secretary of the Convención de Iglesias Menonitas de Puerto Rico. In 2011 Enrique and his wife Kathy moved from the Island to Greencroft Communities in Goshen, Indiana, where Enrique continues to reside.

E arly on, I knew who Enrique Ortiz was and had occasionally spoken with him, but it wasn't until 1973 when he began pastoring my home congregation in Aibonito that I had the pleasure of getting to know him better. From the start, Enrique showed that a service orientation was a strong characteristic of his personality. At around that time I was needing help in remodeling a house on campus at the Academia Menonita Betania, where my family and I were going to be living for my new position as director. Enrique helped me for a number of weeks, without remuneration, until we completed that project.

It was during our many conversations in those weeks that I got to know more about him personally. He attended services and was converted in the Mennonite church near his home in 1950, which incidentally has made him one of the first Puerto Ricans on the Island to become affiliated with the denomination. He grew up in *barrio* Pedro García of the town of Coamo and eventually became pastor of the Aibonito Mennonite church for more than 17 years. He then pastored the Mennonite Church in Summit Hills Church for about five years and served as the Executive Secretary of the Convention of Mennonite Churches of Puerto Rico for six years.

I left the Island in 1976, and then returned for a sabbatical in 1989. Enrique was still a pastor in Aibonito. That year we resumed our friendship and started doing things together, and his penchant for serving others came to the fore again. If I needed a mechanic and gave him a call, my good friend Enrique was there with his tools, ready to help without charging a dime. When I had to go to Caguas to see the chiropractor, Enrique was there to accompany me. Then when I changed to a chiropractor in Ponce, he good-naturedly joined me, even though the distance was further and the trips quite regular. At times, accompanied by his beloved wife Kathy and members of my family, we would also plan day trips, exploring favorite or new-to-us places of the Island together.

Time has passed, and some years later, now in Goshen, Indiana, our paths have come together again. At this writing, we even live very close, actually a couple of blocks from each other. Every month we get together as charter members of a group of Puerto Rican Mennonite retirees, affectionately called the Boricua Boys. Here, Enrique and I have the opportunity to share during and after the meetings. But it does not stop there. Periodically one of us will give the other a call, and in our long conversations we explore topics such as what is going on in our beloved Island, what is happening with the Cubs, and any news and reflections we may have on the Mennonite Church in the USA and Puerto Rico.

Without any doubt in my mind, my good friend, "*el jíbaro de Pedro García*," as I affectionately call him, is worthy of admiration for his great commitment to the Mennonite Church, its beliefs and his years-long support and service to its community. In other words, Enrique Ortiz merits inclusion as we speak of the pillars of the Mennonite work in Puerto Rico.

Rafael Falcón

18

JOSÉ M. ORTIZ

José M. Ortiz was a teacher in Academia Menonita Betania and in Academia Menonita Summit Hills. He worked as pastor in La Cuchilla and Summit Hills Mennonite churches. After moving to the States he served in the Office of Latin Concerns with the General Board of the Mennonite Church. He also taught at Goshen College, Goshen, Indiana, and in Eastern Mennonite Seminary, Harrisonburg, Virginia. Before he retired, he worked for Mennonite Central Committee USA from 1999 to 2004. José currently lives in Goshen with his wife Iraida Rivera.

T here are so many people who José touched when he was in the ministry. Many of the leaders who helped him are gone. Only a few remain, so they can't share about his life and the work of the church. He loved the church while he was a preacher in Palo Hincado. He at times became discouraged but he would say, "God is good, we need to trust Him." He dedicated most of his life to the work of the church

Now that he is retired, he lives with his memories and the love for church and family. You can see it when you read his books and the articles that he so much enjoyed writing.

Consuelo Ortiz Brenner

J osé's life is characterized by the many lives he touched, guided, and nurtured. His everyday life and career mirrored his professional life. My brother has always been intrigued with seeds, plants and trees. He planted the seeds, and loved to see them grow, mature, and produce.

As a pastor, teacher, and counselor he saw his students like seeds in need of guidance, nurturing, and stability. He touched the lives of many young people from Latin America, Mexico, and Puerto Rico.

He was a product of Mennonite higher education, studying at Hesston College, Goshen College, and Mennonite seminaries, where he gave lectures and taught theology courses. He is highly educated but very approachable and caring.

In Puerto Rico he served as a pastor in several Mennonite churches, where his legacy and influence is still felt, and many lasting friendships were made.

The Mennonite General Board offered him a position in the States working with the Latino population within the Mennonite Church. This was a permanent move, but his heart was always in Puerto Rico. He visited the island often, preaching, teaching, and recruiting students to study at our Mennonite institutions.

His biggest influence has been working with young students preparing for the ministry and taking many of them under his wing. Many times he went to the bank to get money to help with

131

tuition and books.

In spite of setbacks, some forms of discrimination, and economic ups and downs, he still remained optimistic. He gave his talents, time, and energy to the life of the Mennonite Church. This is his legacy plus the books and the many articles he wrote. He is very well respected and loved by all the lives he has touched in so many different situations and places. José M. Ortiz is a Christian role model and beacon of light.

Elena Ortiz Hershberger

19

FIDEL SANTIAGO

Fidel was born on December 8, 1926 in Certejenas, *barrio* La Plata de Aibonito, in Puerto Rico. After two years of 1-W service in the La Plata Mennonite Hospital, Fidel took a course in X-ray Technique, and then worked as an X-ray technician at the Tuberculosis Sanatorium in Cayey. He served as pastor of the Cayey Mennonite church while Paul Lauver was on furlough. He also served as an announcer for Audición Luz y Verdad. After obtaining his BA and then his Master's degree in Social Work, Fidel practiced social work in Cayey, Cidra, Caguas, and Comerío.

In 1982 he and Patricia moved to California, where he worked for 17 years as a salesman at the Forrest Lawn Memorial Park in Glendale, California. In 2001 he and Patricia retired and moved to Harrisonburg, then to Lancaster, where they live in Woodcrest Villa, an independent living facility.

⸺⸺◦◦⸺⸺

What did it mean for Fidel Santiago to become a Puerto Rican Mennonite? What defined him as a Puerto Rican Mennonite? Was he a typical Puerto Rican Mennonite? This story has answers to these questions, and it will hopefully raise additional questions about what it means to become a Puerto Rican Mennonite.

Early Life Before Contact with Mennonites (1926-1942)

Fidel was born in a remote sector of *barrio* La Plata of Aibonito called Certenejas, located on the hills that jutted into the confluence of Río Usabón and Río La Plata. Along the sloping hills of Certenejas which bordered Cidra to the east and Barranquitas to the west, his father, who was also called Fidel, took care of the family farmland, where green tobacco plants dotted the hilly landscape.

He was the fifth child in a family of seven. He remembers that his family was poor. Their meals consisted of *funche, sopa de leche,* rice and beans, *verduras,* milk from a family cow, eggs from home grown chickens, and occasionally chicken meat. His mother Elena tended zealously after her *finquita,* where she grew *guineos, plátanos, batatas, yautía, apio,* corn, and other vegetables. With mother Elena, who was firmly in charge of the household, the family always had enough to eat.

He and his older sister Ana Matilde attended first grade through third grade in a one-room school house in La Parada, another sector of La Plata, about a mile or two from his home. A farmhand took Fidel and Ana Matilde to school every day in *banastas* that hung from the back of his family's donkey. In first grade, Fidel had a good teacher whose name was Rafael Ortiz. His spouse, who also taught at the school, was not so nice. She once hit Fidel in the face because he had forgotten to bring his pencil.

His father lost the Certenejas farm because he could not pay the taxes that had accumulated over the years. The family had to move in with another family in Certenejas. This was difficult for his mother to handle. Eventually the family moved for one year to a house owned by Elena's sister in barrio Caonillas of Aibonito.

After the year in Caonillas, the family moved back to La Plata to a house in El Peñón, another sector of *barrio* La Plata located along Road #14. Road #14, or Carretera Central, was an engineering marvel at the time it was built in the late 1800s. It represented an infrastructure legacy that the Spaniards left for Puerto Rico which to this day provides transportation access to many towns and *barrios* across the south central mountains of the island.

The family moved to El Peñón because his father had been asked to serve as *mayordomo* of a farm along the La Plata River, which was down the hill from the house. Fidel's mother sold clandestine *pitrinche* (moonshine) to people who worked for his father. After the workers got paid, they would buy *pitrinche* from his mother. She kept the three or four gallons of *pitrinche* well-hidden, and when authorities arrived, they could not find them.

For his fourth-grade year, Fidel attended Segunda Unidad de La Plata, which was newly built in 1936 with funds from the Puerto Rico Reconstruction Administration (PRRA), President Roosevelt's New Deal program that benefitted the impoverished island. The school was not far from his home in El Peñón. He could walk to it. He recalls that María Teresa Martínez was a young and pretty fourth grade teacher whom he liked. She taught him English and Arithmetic. His books were in English, which he did not understand.

In intermediate school he took an Industrial Arts class under Mr. Rafael Olazagasti' who was originally from the town of Guayama. Fidel remembers building an armchair as a class project. He also took an agricultural class with Mr. Fernando del Río. One day, Mr. Del Río asked him to memorize a speech for an oratorical competition between schools in the region, such as those in Toíta of Cayey and Bayamoncito of Cidra. He earned second prize. As a reward Mr. Del Río took Fidel with him to his home in Añasco, on the western part of the island. On their way through Ponce, Fidel saw the ocean for the first time in his life, and he exclaimed: *"¡qué canto 'e chalco!"*

Fidel's family was nominally Catholic. They attended church once a year during Holy Week. On occasion, his mother gathered the family in the evenings and recited the rosary in Latin. Everyone had to be quiet. She also reached out to *santeros* when family members fell ill. For example, his father suffered from back aches. They called a *santero* who performed a *ventosa* over his father's back. The *ventosa* consisted of placing a drinking glass over a candle set on top of the skin, and then running the heated glass across the back.

Fidel was about 14 years old when the family moved to a *parcela* in La Plata, near the cone-shaped hill in the center of the La Plata Valley that was commonly known as *La Lomita*. His father bought the *parcela* for $35. A *parcela* came with a concrete house that included two small bedrooms and a small living room. My father slept in the living room with his father. His older sisters Elena, Isabel, and Ana Matilde slept in one of the bedrooms, and his mother and younger sister Elisa slept in the other bedroom. The *parcela* also came with five *cuerdas* of land. A *cuerda* is a measure of land smaller than an acre. *Parcelas* were constructed and distributed to farmers during a land distribution effort of the New Deal programs of the 1930s. Fidel's father grew sugar cane on the five *cuerdas* spread along the hillside of *La Lomita*.

Engaging With Mennonites During Initial Years (1943-1950)

Wilbur Nachtigall and Justus Holsinger were the first two Mennonite Civilian Public Service (CPS) workers Fidel met after they arrived in La Plata on July 19, 1943. They lived in a bunk house which was not far from the *parcela* where Fidel lived. Fidel was 16 years-old at the time. Fidel remembers some of the early experiences with the CPSers, such as taking a long walk to the town of Comerío and exploring a cave called Cueva de la Mora

136

that was full of bats. As time went by, he became good friends with service workers like Addona Nissley and Floyd Zehr.

Lester Hershey and his family arrived in La Plata in April of 1947. Lester became the first Mennonite pastor in La Plata. Shortly after arrival, Lester invited Fidel to church activities. It didn't take long before Fidel decided he would no longer smoke cigarettes after he found out that smoking was incompatible with his newly found Mennonite faith and lifestyle. In 1948, he was baptized at the new Mennonite congregation together with Samuel Rolón, doña Juana Rolón, Esteban Rivera, and Carmen Camacho. Fidel was 21 years old when he became a member of the Iglesia Menonita del Calvario, five years after the first Mennonites arrived in La Plata.

Fidel graduated from Aibonito High School in May, 1946. He was 19 years old at the time. In 1947, the Experimental Station of the University of Puerto Rico hired Fidel to serve in an egg improvement project. He tended after different types of hens, one of which was white leghorn. He was trying to identify which type of hen laid the best eggs. The project contained 16 large cages. Fidel gathered eggs from the hen in each cage. A hen laid the egg in a box from which it could not escape. After the egg was laid, Fidel would label the egg with the number of the hen and then let the hen out of the box. He worked about three years on the project until 1949, when it moved to Lajas, a town in the southwest part of the island.

Conscientious Objector (1951-1956)

In the early 1950s the U.S. Selective Service System called Fidel to serve in the armed forces during the Korean War. Fidel decided to become a conscientious objector to war. Lester Hershey supported him and accompanied him to his interview before the draft board. The board granted him his request. With his new 1-W status in hand, he went on to perform civilian service for two years as a receptionist at the Mennonite General Hospital in La Plata. He remained there until 1956.

In the summer of 1954, he met Patricia Ann Brenneman at a prayer meeting in La Plata. Patricia was on vacation from her teaching job in Sarasota, Florida, visiting with her friends Martha Kanagy and Doris Snyder. Patricia was wearing a yellow dress. Fidel never forgot that.

Fidel and Patricia exchanged letters frequently between Florida and Puerto Rico throughout the 1954-55 school year. During that year, Patricia applied to become a missionary teacher at the Escuela Menonita Betania in Puerto Rico through Mennonite Board of Missions and Charities. She was accepted, and during the 1956-57 school year she taught a joint third and fourth grade class at Betania. Among her students were Carolyn Holderread, Rafael Falcón, Tom Lehman, Benjamín Colón, and Alwin González. Fidel and Patricia continued their courtship that year, and this time they could actually spend time together as a couple or with groups of their Mennonite friends, rather than writing to each other.

Tuberculosis (TB) was a major public health challenge in Puerto Rico in 1950, accounting for 128 deaths per 100,000 in the population. The TB mortality rate in Puerto Rico was almost six times higher than on the U.S. mainland. The federally funded Operation Bootstrap during the governorship of Luis Muñoz Marín included public health projects aimed at combatting TB. In 1955, Fidel took a course called X-ray Technique at the Modern Tabulating and Technology School in San Juan. Taking the course in San Juan required him to live in the metropolitan area. Bob Ehret, the owner of Ehret Funeral Home in San Juan and a former CPSer, invited him to stay at his facilities. Fidel took an X-ray technician licensing exam in Ponce in the first part of 1956.

The X-ray Technician Years (1957-1963)
On June 8, 1956, Timothy H. Brenneman, Patricia's father, who was pastor of Bay Shore Mennonite Church in Sarasota, Florida, married Patricia and Fidel at the Bay Shore Mennonite Church. During their honeymoon Fidel received a telegraph from his sister Elena indicating that he had received a letter inviting him to an interview for an X-ray technician position with a physician in San Juan by the name of Dr. Padró. He and Patricia cut their honeymoon short and returned to Puerto Rico for the interview.

Shortly after, Fidel was hired to serve at the Tuberculosis Sanatorium in Cayey with a salary of $140 a month.

During his first year of marriage, Fidel co-pastored the emerging Mennonite church in Guavate. Fidel and Patricia's first son Rolando was born in the spring of 1957. Many years later Rolando married Raquel Trinidad, whose mother Modesta Martínez attended the Guavate congregation in 1956 when Fidel was co-pastoring. It's very likely that Modesta and Patricia worshipped together at that time when both were pregnant of Raquel and Rolando.

In 1958 Fidel was asked to move to the parsonage in Cayey and pastor the congregation for a year while missionary Paul Lauver and his family were on furlough in the United States. During this time, Fidel continued his full-time job as X-ray technician in Cayey and his second son, Ricardo, was born. He also served as an announcer for the Audición Luz y Verdad, a Mennonite evangelistic radio broadcast for Latin America.

After the year in Cayey, they moved back to La Plata and they bought a house that had been used for medical personnel at the Mennonite General Hospital, but was no longer needed for this purpose since the hospital had moved to Aibonito in 1957.

The Social Work Years (1964-1981)
During his eight years as X-ray technician, Fidel took evening and weekend courses toward a bachelor's degree in elementary education at the Inter American University Campus in Cayey. He was awarded a BA at graduation ceremonies on May 3, 1964 at the San Germán Campus. Earlier in the year, he had also been awarded a teaching certificate from the Department of Public Instruction of Puerto Rico. However, he never taught school.

That was because in 1964, Mrs. Loyola, a woman with influence in the Puerto Rico government, encouraged him to apply for a position in social services. This was the same year when President Johnson's War on Poverty legislation was being enacted in Congress. Fidel started to work as a *trabajador de asistencia a la familia* (TABF) in Aguas Buenas.

In 1971, Fidel was offered the opportunity to earn his master's degree in social work while still receiving a full-time salary. He availed himself of this opportunity. During his first year of coursework at the Río Piedras Campus of the University of Puerto Rico, he stayed at the house in Reparto Metropolitano where his mother, sister, and nephew were living. He graduated on May 29th, 1973.

Fidel practiced social work in Cayey, Cidra, Caguas, and Comerío. After 30 years of government service, he was eligible for a government pension and retired in 1982. His last social work position was in Comerío and Barranquitas, where he served as a supervising social worker in the Women, Infants, and Children (WIC) program.

During the 1960s and 1970s Fidel and his family were active members of Mennonite congregations in La Plata, Cidra, and Aibonito. In La Plata, Fidel served as treasurer of the congregation for some years. He also served on the board of Academia Menonita Betania for some time while his children attended the school.

Migrating to the States (1982 Onward)

The summer of 1981 was a shocker for Fidel and Patricia when they lost their son Ricardo in a tragic car accident. The emotional impact of their son's death led Fidel and Patricia to sell their home in La Plata and move to Los Angeles, California, where two of Fidel's sisters lived. Once in California, Fidel began treatment for dermatomyositis, a rare disease affecting the muscles of the body. If untreated, the disease could be fatal. Fidel received treatment at the University of California Los Angeles (UCLA) Medical Campus. The treatment turned out to be very effective, and the disease was eradicated from his body, never to return. He then began a 17-year second career at Forrest Lawn Memorial Park in Glendale, California, as a before-need salesperson. He was successful selling memorial property, and for two years received the "salesman of the year" award.

In 2001, Fidel and Patricia retired to Harrisonburg, Virginia, where their good friends Mary and Addona Nissley lived. They became members of Park View Mennonite Church. In 2004, they moved to an independent living apartment at Virginia Mennonite Retirement Community, where they remained until 2018, when they moved to another independent living apartment at Woodcrest Villa in Lancaster, Pennsylvania. Once in Lancaster they attended Neffsville Mennonite Church. In Lancaster, they also lived close to their son Rolando and his spouse, Raquel, and their grandson Jared's family, and enjoyed many joyful family gatherings.

Rolando Santiago

20

CLARA SPRINGER

Clara Unzicker Springer lived and worked in Puerto Rico, along with her husband Elmer Springer, for several decades. As one of the early Mennonite workers, she used her gifts in a variety of ways, primarily in education. She was instrumental in the establishment of the Escuela Menonita Betania in 1947, and was later an appreciated teacher for many children through her Sunday school classes.

———◦———

C lara was born in Fisher, Illinois on February 6, 1909. She passed away in Glendale, Arizona, on February 20, 2004.

She married Elmer R. Springer on December 26, 1929 in Fisher, Illinois. After marrying Elmer, Clara was a teacher in various rural schools for more than 10 years. After that, she worked in the office of a tractor and farm implement business started by her husband.

In 1946 Elmer and Clara were called by the Mennonite Church Mission Board to go to work for a year in Puerto Rico. In the summer of 1946 they answered the call and, together with their son Fred, left their family and their business in Illinois and traveled by cargo ship to Puerto Rico to work on a new project established in Pulguillas. During this first year they worked with Paul Lauver and his wife Lois to establish a new Mennonite church and build several homes and other buildings needed in the project. Paul knew Spanish, as he had lived in Argentina as a child, but the others learned Spanish day by day during their work on the project with the local people. During this time Clara worked mainly with the children in Sunday schools and other services during the week.

With the church established and growing every day, it was time to establish a school. Elmer and Clara felt called to continue their work in Puerto Rico rather than return to Illinois. Beulah Litwiller came to Pulguillas to work with the other workers. She was fluent in Spanish, having lived in Argentina as a child, and was very supportive of the mission's work. During the summer of 1947 Clara and Beulah crisscrossed the mountains of the Pulguillas neighborhood inviting the children of the local families to attend a new school that was being started.

In August of that year the first and second grades of the new Christian school at Pulguillas were established. The school shared space in the original church building until the new church was built. Clara taught English, arithmetic, and social studies classes and Beulah taught the classes that required a better knowledge of Spanish.

Each year another grade was added to accommodate students progressing through their studies. Carol Glick and Anna K.

Massanari came to teach, and other teachers were also added as the school grew.

With the school well established, Clara and Elmer moved to missionary work in Palo Hincado and Cuchilla. Her second son Ted (or "Teddy", as he was known in Puerto Rico.) had been born in La Plata in 1950. Her eldest son, Fred, returned to the United States to continue his studies.

They later returned to Aibonito to work with the Ulrich Foundation at the beginning of that project. They worked there until they returned to the United States and moved to Goshen, Indiana. In all, they worked in Puerto Rico for 24 years.

Surely Clara did not understand in 1946 the magnitude of the work ahead when she left her well-established life in Illinois to live with her family in a foreign country without knowing the language. Simply, along with her husband and son, they responded to serve in the work to which God called them. From that day on, a long line of teachers, workers and administrators dedicated to the same vision has followed until today—the vision of integrating Christian faith and academic knowledge in the lives of students, to develop people capable of being useful to their communities and the world at large.

Ted Springer

21

GEORGE D. TROYER

George D. Troyer (1890-1969) was a medical missionary in India and Puerto Rico. He was born February 26, 1890 in Howard County, Indiana, the fifteenth child born to the Old Mennonite farming family of John Troyer and Caroline Shrock, his second wife. George was the last of John Troyer's twenty-nine children to reach adulthood and the only one to attend college. He graduated from Marion Normal College, a teachers' college, and taught school between 1912 and 1916. He married Kathryn Sommers on

July 12, 1914. Together the young couple took the radical decision of moving with their infant son Nortell to Chicago so George could enter Chicago Medical School, which allowed employed men and women to study medicine at night. To support his family George worked as a conductor on the elevated train, among other jobs. Son Dana and daughter Annabelle were born at this time. George graduated from medical school in 1922.

On November 10, 1923, Dr. George Troyer and his young family left New York aboard the *S.S. Albania* on the first leg of a trip bound for India, where the Mennonite Board of Missions had sent them as medical missionaries. The family spent thirteen venturesome years in India. Dr. Troyer served as medical director of Dhamtari Christian Hospital part of that time. Son Weldon was born in India in 1933. Following a bout with malaria, and possibly as a result of quinine toxicity, Dr. Troyer suffered from hearing loss the rest of his life. The Troyer family circumnavigated the globe twice on trips to and from India.

The Troyers returned to the United States in 1936, settling in Fisher, Illinois for eight years, where Dr. Troyer developed an interest in ophthalmology. In 1944 the Mennonite Relief Committee recommended sending him to Puerto Rico to investigate the possibility of medical work there. Asked to give a year's service to the Mennonite Central Committee unit in La Plata, Dr. Troyer joined the unit in December, 1944. The following year he helped scout for locations in the Pulguillas community suitable for a school, church and clinic. In August, 1945, Don Antonio "El Corso" Emanuelli agreed to deed ten acres of his land for the purpose. The Betania church and school still stand on this site. Dr. Troyer also bought a small farm in Pulguillas. One of the earliest commercial poultry-raising projects in the community was established there. Dr. Troyer and wife Kathryn were also catalysts in convincing their friends, the Ray Ulrich family, to begin the important Ulrich Foundation project in Aibonito. In 1951 Dr. Troyer was named medical director of the Mennonite Medical Program in Puerto Rico. During the years he was affiliated with the Mennonite Hospital and later in private practice, Dr. Troyer earned renown on the island as a skilled eye surgeon, specializing in cataract surgery. In the mid-50s Dr. Troyer added an eye clinic to a large house he had purchased in the Campito section of Aibonito. In the basement of the house Nortell, his son, ground the corrective lenses prescribed by Dr. Troyer. In the 1960's he travelled several times to the neighboring islands of Nevis and St. Kitts to provide his services there.

Dr. Troyer was also an ordained minister. He officiated the first wedding celebrated in the new church in La Plata in 1946, marrying his daughter Annabelle to Lawrence Greaser. Dr. George Delton Troyer died December 6, 1969 at Goshen, Indiana, completing an improbable journey from the cornfields of Indiana to the medical fields of India and Puerto Rico, where thousands of the sick and needy benefitted from his desire to serve others. A street in Aibonito near the Mennonite Hospital was named in his honor.

———————

M y grandfather, George Troyer, was a man of many gifts and talents. By the time he, Kathryn and their youngest son, Weldon, arrived in Puerto Rico in 1944, he had taught school, studied for his medical degree and a specialty in ophthalmology, had been a medical missionary in India for 13 years, and had a private practice in Fisher, Illinois.

In Puerto Rico, while working at the hospital in La Plata, he was asked to start a mission. He was a pioneer, as he negotiated for the land in Pulguillas that later became Escuela Menonita Betania and Betania Mennonite Church. He had a small farm in Pulguillas with oranges, coffee, bananas and chickens as a way of providing jobs and doing development in the community. The road to the farm was steep and curvy. Because of George's hearing loss, he had trouble knowing when to shift the gears and could be heard from a distance gunning it up the mountain. One didn't want to be behind the vehicle when he started driving, as it spewed gravel everywhere.

I also saw a side of Grandpa besides the doctor, statesman,

preacher and pioneer. I saw the man who loved to sing the songs of his youth like "When Johnny comes marching home again, hurrah, hurrah" sung loudly, as it didn't sound loud to him. I saw his love of humor and remember the can of "peanuts" at their house that had a spring-loaded snake inside that would pop up when the lid was taken off. I knew the man who made origami swans and who helped Grandma recycle materials from the glove factory in Aibonito to make rag rugs. As I sat next to him in church, Grandpa taught me how to make paper boats out of the bulletin and babies in the blanket with his handkerchief. Grandma was busy writing down the sermon in English for him to read later, so Grandpa had time to entertain me during the sermon.

Dr. George Troyer was a strong man of conviction and passion and he was also humble and gentle. After being poked with a dull needle by him when I needed my smallpox shot, I wasn't so sure I wanted to sit by him. My mother was not happy with me and said, "Your Grandpa wouldn't hurt a flea." He was a man of compassion who healed many people, removed many cataracts and performed other specialized eye treatments that were not otherwise available in central Puerto Rico. He visited people in communities that could only be reached by horseback. He shared the Gospel in word and deed and helped lead and shape the new Mennonite Church and the Mennonite Hospital in Puerto Rico.

I am very thankful for my grandfather and the strong spiritual and Godly legacy he left behind. He was a strong man with many professional skills which he used to serve and bless others. His life was built on the rock of Jesus Christ and when the storms of life came he stood firm.

Rachel Greaser Good

When Dr. George D. Troyer arrived in Puerto Rico with his family in December 1944, he was sent and sponsored by the Mennonite Board of Missions and Charities of Elkhart, Indiana, but worked under the auspices and control of Mennonite Central Committee to provide health care, along with two other Mennonite doctors, at the Civilian Public Service hospital in La Plata, Puerto Rico. His mandate from the Mission Board was to look for the possibility of beginning mission work in that area of Puerto Rico.

After consulting with the leaders of the CPS unit, and also after speaking with other Protestant church leaders in nearby areas, he was invited to look for a parcel of land by a local landowner, Don Antonio Emanuelli, who had been treated at the Mennonite Hospital in La Plata.[1]

Meanwhile the excellent health care and health education provided by the members of the CPS unit at the Mennonite Hospital in La Plata had been steadily extended to surrounding communities. From 1945 to 1951, medical outpatient clinics were established in Buena Vista and Toíta in Cayey, Rabanal and Salto in Cidra, and Betania and Coamo Arriba in Barrio Pulguillas. Dr. Troyer and the other doctors from La Plata covered these outpatient clinics, as well as the regular outpatient clinics held daily at the La Plata Hospital.

Along with these health clinics, milk stations were begun in March 1957 in Pulguillas and other clinics to provide milk for needy children. A dental clinic was added one day a week, with Dr. Earl Stover, dentist, providing that important service. Dr. Troyer continued working at the La Plata Mennonite Hospital, as well as conducting day clinics in Pulguillas and having a private ophthalmology clinic in his home in Pulguillas. In 1952 Dr. Troyer wrote in his annual report to the Mission Board that with regard to home deliveries in the Pulguillas area, mothers in labor were having their babies at home without medical assistance because the nurses and doctor were not able to get to their homes in time. This condition was becoming more acute in Pulguillas. He was also being called out more often to treat other diseases, due to the distance those patients were from the municipal hospitals. "Many are the disparaging remarks one hears concerning governmental hospitals which are often understaffed and overcrowded. The government, however, is doing everything it can to cope with the ever increasing population. The new Mennonite Hospital that we are looking forward to building in the near future in Aibonito, cannot come too soon to serve the people in a better way, and will certainly be a great blessing to the community. Recently we were approached by the Puerto Rican doctor in charge of the government Health Centers in the Coamo District, asking if we could possibly help out by taking over the Pulguillas Health Center. The doctor who had been in charge of this clinic recently left the work. All that I could promise was that if and when another doctor comes to help us on our work, we might be able to arrange something." [2]

As plans moved forward, it became obvious that a new hospital had to be constructed, since the current hospital building in La Plata had been condemned by Insular health officials, making it necessary to operate under a provisional license.

In May 1951, Dr. Troyer successfully passed the medical licensure exam in Puerto Rico and received his license as physician and surgeon. In June of that year the Mission Board appointed him Medical Director of the Mennonite Hospital in Puerto Rico and Dr. Walter Massanari as Assistant Director. As medical director, Dr. Troyer was delegated to be the Mission Board's representative for all health care decisions. He soon found out that the power-of-attorney he was using was not sufficient for obtaining what was needed, so he wrote to Elkhart detailing the wording that was required for the work he was doing.

In September 1953, the Mission Board sent a letter to Dr. Troyer including the following: "The Board of Mennonite Missions and Charities appoints Dr. George D. Troyer M.D. our True and Lawful Attorney, with power and authority to sign...... all applications, forms, reports, and statements related to applications made to the Insular Government of Puerto Rico or to the Federal Government at Washington, D.C., relative to receiving sanction for building and Government aid for said Hospital building, and equipment for a Hospital to be built by the Board at Aibonito, Puerto Rico." It was signed by J.D. Graber, Secretary.[3]

A building committee was formed and chaired by Luke Birky. A plot of land was donated by Raymond Ulrich through the

Ulrich Foundation. It was located on the northwest outskirts of Aibonito, near an elementary school. An architect was chosen to draw up the plans for the hospital, and construction bids were opened in July 1955. A contractor was chosen to build the new 32 bed hospital at an estimated cost of $415,000. Of this amount the Federal Hill-Burton Act would contribute two thirds, or about $276,668, leaving $138,332 to be raised by private contributions.

At the annual meeting of the Mission Board in 1956, the Puerto Rico report on the medical work in La Plata revealed that 10,474 patients had been treated in the outpatient clinic at the hospital, making it all the more important to quickly begin construction of the new Aibonito hospital.[4]

The ground breaking ceremony for the new Aibonito hospital took place on Saturday, July 23, 1955. The money to fund the proposed new hospital building project was solicited from members of the Mennonite congregations in Puerto Rico and the United States and Canada. They also came from the city of Aibonito and surrounding areas, and finally from the larger San Juan metropolitan area.

Two individuals who led the way in fund raising were Luke Birky and John Lehman. John did most of his solicitation by mail, but also met with many different individuals and groups. One such group was arranged by the wife of Governor Luis Muñoz Marín, Doña Inés María Mendoza. John Lehman was invited to attend a dinner meeting at La Fortaleza to which many of the people interested in the new hospital had been invited. His presentation resulted in pledges of over $90,000 for the hospital.

Luke Birky left his family in Puerto Rico for eight months while he traveled all over the United States and Canada visiting different Mennonite churches and organizations, fund raising for the hospital. These months of separation from his family were difficult, but resulted in helping to raise the necessary funds to build the new hospital.

Meanwhile, in Aibonito a fund raising committee was formed for soliciting from business and community leaders. Juan Negrón became the chair of this committee, and the Aibonito community responded with great enthusiasm. The Mennonite Hospital inauguration ceremony occurred on Sunday, March 24, 1957, and the hospital began to offer health services the next day.

Some of the leaders at the ceremony were Lester Hershey, President of the Mennonite Churches of Puerto Rico; Dr. George D. Troyer, Medical Director; Dr. Herbert Neff, Hospital administrator; Dr. Juan A. Pons, head of the Puerto Rico Department of Health; Judge A. Cecil Snyder, President of the Supreme Court of Puerto Rico; Ernesto Ramos Antonini, Speaker of the House of Representatives; and Juan Negrón, chair of the Aibonito committee pro Mennonite Hospital.

As I write this in 2020, 76 years have passed since the rural hospital in the La Plata valley began its service, and 63 years since the Aibonito hospital was dedicated. Since that time, many hands and hearts have continued to contribute to this endeavor of advancement and improvement of the quality of health in Puerto Rico.

If you would ask a person on the street in Puerto Rico what the word Menonita signifies for them, you would probably hear them say "excellent and caring health service." Large bill boards in Caguas, Cayey and Aibonito carry this message to the public, as well as frequent announcements on television and radio.

Mennonite Health System now manages six hospitals in central Puerto Rico: Aibonito, Cayey, Caguas, Humacao, Guayama, and CIMA, a psychiatric facility. In addition it staffs outpatient clinics and provides 24/7 emergency medicine services in Aguas Buenas, Barranquitas, Cidra, Coamo, Comerío and Orocovis.

Mennonite Health System is the third largest health care provider in Puerto Rico and employs over 2,800 colleagues, with 600 physicians in all specialties and subspecialties and many volunteers. Their mission is to serve with the Love of Christ to provide integrated, excellent health services to the community with loving care and without discrimination.

I think that Dr. George D. Troyer would say "To GOD be the glory."

Dr. G. Weldon Troyer M.D.

Footnotes:

1. Report of 40th annual meeting of the MBMC, 1946; report from Puerto Rico, p. 16.

2. Report of Annual meeting of the MBMC, 1954, report from Puerto Rico, p. 202

3, Private correspondence from MBMC to Dr. Troyer, Sept. 30, 1953.

4, Report of Annual meeting of the MBMC, 1956, report from Puerto Rico, p. 212.

The writing of this article was greatly assisted by verification of dates and other details from the book: *Sistema de Salud Menonita, una página extraordinaria en la historia de Puerto Rico,* authored by Ana Beatriz Torres Hernández, Published by Disonex, S. A., 2017. ISBN: 978-1-61790-118-8

22

KATHRYN TROYER

Kathryn Sommers (1893-1973) was born September 30, 1893, at Bennetts Switch, Miami County, Indiana, the second of twelve children born to Daniel J. Sommers (1863-1933) and Elizabeth Zook (1873-1953). She left school at an early age to help care for younger siblings. She married George D. Troyer on July 12, 1914. Byron Nortell, their first son, was born in 1918. The young family then made the daunting, life-altering decision to relocate to Chicago so husband George could enter medical school. Dana (1920) and Annabelle (1921) were added to the family while there. To help support the family she embroidered handkerchiefs and took in laundry. The time in Chicago caring for three small children and a medical student, while challenging enough, was scant preamble for what followed. In 1923 the Troyer family left behind the comforts of a familiar world to begin life as medical missionaries in a foreign and distant land. For their thirteen years in India, Kathryn tended to the needs of her growing family, learned Hindi, and led Bible study groups for Indian women. Daughter Louise, born in 1928, died shortly after birth. Son Weldon was born in India in 1933.

Between 1944 and 1967, when the Troyer family lived in Puerto Rico, Kathryn provided invaluable assistance to her husband George. She learned Spanish and was the communication link between patients and Dr. Troyer. His contributions would have been significantly diminished without her capable support. In Puerto Rico she again proved to be an effective leader of women's Bible study groups. She or son Weldon translated Dr. Troyer's sermons for the group that began meeting Sunday mornings in the late 1950s in the Ehret funeral home in Hato Rey. The Bayamón Mennonite Church grew out of this initial small group of families that had moved to the metropolitan area. She was also an unwitting precursor of the flower business in Aibonito. Cultivating her affinity for African violets, she grew them in a small greenhouse and sold them to the public.

When the Troyers retired to Goshen, Indiana in 1967, Kathryn was actively involved with the Hispanic community there and assisted in the beginning of the Iglesia Menonita del Buen Pastor. She died in Goshen on June 16, 1973. The street in Aibonito named for Dr. Troyer could just as aptly have been called the Calle Dr. George Troyer y Kathryn Sommers Troyer.

K athryn Sommers grew up as a neighbor of George Troyer in the farm country of central Indiana. India and Puerto Rico were faraway places that no one in their families had ever imagined visiting, let alone living in. After George and Kathryn were married, she was right beside him as he taught school and enrolled in medical school. Finally the time came for them to serve the church on foreign fields—13 years in India and 23 years in Puerto Rico. They reared four children and also cared for a grandchild for several years.

Kathryn was a person who saw things as black or white. She did not hesitate to call us out if she felt we were straying. But we always knew she loved us and had our best interests in mind. She also had our good health in mind when she used her juicer to make carrot juice or a concoction of fresh vegetables from her garden. For those of us who were not very fond of vegetables it was sometimes a stretch but we tried to taste some to make her happy.

Grandma Troyer also loved plants, especially African violets. She had a greenhouse with many varieties which she loved to share with others. She also excelled in the kitchen, making plenty of food for family meals, whether it was Amish Mennonite favorites when she served mashed potatoes and noodles at the same meal plus pie, or Indian feasts or Puerto Rican cooking. I remember one meal as a child when my eyes were bigger than my stomach and I needed to rest afterward on their big four-poster bed.

Kathryn had a heart for personal evangelism. She loved to visit people and tell them about Jesus, and many came to know Him through her witness. George was hard of hearing because of an overdose of quinine in India to treat his malaria. Because of this, he was not able to learn Spanish. Kathryn worked closely with him as an interpreter as they worked with the church and community or at their eye practice.

Even though she had to drop out of school early to help care for her siblings, Kathryn was fluent in three languages and kept learning and increasing in knowledge on her own. Her worn Bible spoke of her love for God's Word. After suffering a stroke close to the end of her life, Kathryn could not speak well but she could sing the hymns she loved. She asked me to read John 14 to her as she looked forward to being with Jesus in her heavenly home.

Kathryn and George were a team with the goals of serving others, making a difference in their communities, and bringing glory to God. As we look back on their lives, we can see that they met those goals and have heard: "Well done, good and faithful servant... Enter into the joy of your Master." Matthew 25:21.

Rachel Greaser Good

23

RAYMOND ULRICH

Raymond was born April 3, 1912, in Shelbyville, Illinois. As a young man he worked for his brother, who was a mechanic. During this time he invented and patented several devices. Later he founded the Ulrich Manufacturing Co. He married Verda Zoss in 1941. Dr George Troyer invited them to visit Puerto Rico, which they did in 1949. Impressed by the need he saw, he bought land and founded the Ulrich Foundation in Aibonito, Puerto Rico, as an agricultural demonstration project. The Foundation was approved by Selective Service to employ 1-W registrants. He donated the land in Aibonito on which the Mennonite Hospital and the Mennonite Church were built. He passed away on June 26, 2007, in Eureka, Illinois.

———————◦○◦———————

M y memories:
I remember the many times our family took frozen turkeys with us to Puerto Rico at Christmas. All the Foundation families enjoyed a turkey meal on Christmas Day.

I enjoyed celebrating Three Kings' Day.

I remember the many movies and pictures our father took.

When Dad announced to the family that we were going to Puerto Rico, I could hardly wait. I looked forward to seeing my friends who lived in Aibonito and the surrounding area.

It was always fun to see what the little grocery store on the Ulrich Foundation property had on its shelves.

I have many memories of the mobile dental office that Dad sent to Puerto Rico.

Our living room in Roanoke, Illinois, became a boys' or girls' bedroom when Ulrich Foundation families visited us.

Grace Ulrich Becker

M emories of my father, Raymond M. Ulrich as he directed the Ulrich Foundation in Aibonito, Puerto Rico, from 1949 -1976.

1. I knew my dad as a generous giver—with his time and material possessions. I watched him fulfill his vision of creating a business that would sustain a mission outreach, which became the Ulrich Foundation in Aibonito, Puerto Rico. He invested much time in empowering people to be all they could be. He also became a great mentor. His goal was to teach people "how to fish," giving them the opportunity to develop their gifts and talents and become a blessing to others along the way.

2. My father always shared his dreams and aspirations with us six siblings. We were included in making decisions; he valued our

opinions and thoughts. When a new project for the Foundation was in the making, we were always a part of it. One that stands out in my mind was our participation in helping to buy Christmas gifts for each Ulrich Foundation worker and family member. We spent days wrapping all the gifts around the kitchen table and some years made a trip to Puerto Rico to deliver all the gifts and boxes of food to the workers. We also took many turkeys packed in dry ice along with us.

3. My dad always showed compassion and concern in the little details. He cared deeply about each person working for the Foundation. One year he was told that one of the 1-W young men was homesick for the cold and snow. So my dad bought a Styrofoam ball and after a good soaking in water, would freeze the ball over and over again until it resembled a snowball. Along with the turkeys and other meats, the snowball was packed in dry ice for our Christmas trip to Puerto Rico. Dad was the one to throw the snowball at the homesick worker when we arrived in Aibonito, putting a big smile on his face!

Dad would always make sure each Foundation household had enough dishes, silverware, pots and pans, bedding, blankets, etc. to meet their needs. He shipped many boxes to Puerto Rico when a need arose. All of us siblings were part of the process.

He made sure Spanish classes were offered to each Foundation worker during evening hours. Dad also had a concern and burden for the spiritual well-being of each worker. Once a month, on a Friday evening, the Foundation families and 1-W men would gather together for an English fellowship night at the Ulrich Foundation headquarters known as "Aibonito Hall." They would eat together and then have a hymn sing. A pastor or church leader would then share a scripture or give a message to help encourage each one in their spiritual journey.

4. My dad made sure the work of the Ulrich Foundation was recorded for the generations to come and also to inspire others to fulfill their dreams and aspirations. He always had a large movie camera on his shoulder; it went with him wherever he went.

Today we are blessed to have this history and share it with others. The mayor's office in Aibonito now has this history on DVD and has made copies to share with the community. Many of the movies capture glimpses of grandparents and relatives of people living in the area today.

My father also created a magazine called "The Echo," which was published every three or four months, full of pictures and articles of the day-to-day operations of the Ulrich Foundation. It was a wonderful way of keeping everyone informed of the mission work happening in Puerto Rico. These "The Echo" magazines are now a treasure of the history and memories of the Ulrich Foundation we hold dear.

Linda Ulrich Nussbaum

Our first trip to Puerto Rico was in January 1949. Dr. George Troyer picked up our family, along with Grandma Zoss, at the San Juan International Airport at Isla Grande. All the roads were wet and there were even some puddles, but the sun was shining and there was not a cloud in the sky. My dad asked Dr. Troyer if they had just washed the streets, and he told Dad that it had just rained. As a kid I was impressed that we were riding in a Plymouth and the hood ornament was a sailing ship.

Dad had worked out a deal with the J.C. Penney store in Peoria, Illinois, for them to donate all returns and end of season clothing to the Ulrich Foundation. We would drive to Peoria to pick them up. They had big boxes in a room filled with clothing. We took the boxes home to repack for shipment to Dr. Troyer in Pulguillas, Puerto Rico. We did this two times. One time I remember being in Puerto Rico at Dr. Troyer's home when there was a long line of people going up to the Troyer's back porch to get free clothing.

The Ulrich Foundation had a cattle breeding program in Asomante which was used to upgrade the native herds, as well as the Foundation's. This was done by having frozen semen sent from the Northern Ohio Breeder's Association to the airport in San Juan, then flown to the Asomante farm by small airplane. The plane would fly over the farm and drop the box attached to a small parachute. We loved to run and get the box and put it right into the freezer. My father involved us kids in many aspects of the Foundation's work.

Dad purchased a trailer with the inside unfinished. He had it parked in the shop that was connected to our house in Roanoke, Illinois. There we added dental equipment. As kids we used to play in the trailer and watched it being transformed into a dental office on wheels. My father then had it shipped to Puerto Rico. The dentist office on wheels was pulled to the schools in the Aibonito area to give free dental care to children. It was a great blessing to many.

Richard Ulrich

24

GLADYS WIDMER

Gladys Widmer was born in Noble, Iowa, in 1915. After graduation in 1942 from Goshen College she taught school and then worked for five years as an office assistant at the former Mennonite Board of Missions, a predecessor agency of Mennonite Mission Network.

All along she knew her true calling was to be a missionary, and in fact, her first appointment in that role was to serve in Puerto Rico. Being a single woman missionary in the 1950s was no easy task, and Widmer often found herself stepping out of traditional gender roles to preach and plant churches. Though her initial assignment had been as a teacher, Widmer ultimately started numerous congregations in Puerto Rico during her 30 years of service there.

For her work in the United States, she received the Lark Award in 1995 for church planting. In retirement, Widmer used her knowledge of Spanish to minister to the needs of the growing Hispanic population in Goshen, Indiana. Gladys Widmer died in 2006.

I learned to know Gladys Widmer in 1977. It was my last year at the university and I had gone through a deep existential dilemma which led me to a conversion to Jesus Christ. I started to attend the Mennonite Church in Ponce. Since it was a small church, after receiving several Bible studies I started to assume a leadership role, especially in preaching. In my first preaching experience Gladys prepared the biblical passage and the content of the sermon. My feet trembled, but Gladys offered me good support. In my second sermon she offered me again the biblical text and the content of the sermon. This time the difference was that I chose another biblical passage and I changed the content of the sermon a little bit. At the end, Gladys told me, "You are not being a good disciple." I responded, "If you know more than me, why don't you do it?" She answered, "Women can't preach." I told her, "But you can guide me in my sermon, which for me means that it's like you are the one preaching." She was perturbed a bit by my answer, and it was on that occasion that our commonalities and differences began.

Something that I always remember about Gladys was her love for neighbor and for "souls." For example, there was a time when the motorcycle I used for transportation broke down, and I was left without transportation. She was always available to pick me up at my home, take me to church and then bring me back home. This demonstrated to me that I was important to her, for which I am eternally grateful. This helped my own self esteem because it was spiritually important to her and it helped me explore more the importance of supporting others.

I remember that one Saturday we started to make visits at 10:00 a.m. By 4:00 p.m. I started to feel hungry, since I had not eaten breakfast that day. I told her, "Gladys, can we take a break?" She told me: "The kingdom of God never takes a break." On the one side, her answer bothered me since she didn't seem to empathize with my hunger, but on the other side I admired her love for evangelism. She taught me that her commitment to evangelize happened in season and out of season, and that was non-negotiable. She taught me that no matter our differences in age, culture, place of birth, and vision for the world, we could communicate and find each other creatively in the One who was crucified. In my heart I keep thanking God for Gladys Widmer for being an extraordinary human being with her lights and shadows, and for allowing our spiritual journeys to coincide. We'll see you soon, Gladys ...

Luis Elier Rodríguez

I was born and raised in a public housing project. Economic and social limitations were real. I always had many questions in my mind that needed answers. In 1976, I returned to the university after a voluntary recess. I remember listening to a JELAM radio program and decided to write and ask about what was tormenting me at that moment. Honestly, I never expected a response. That was a time when people wrote letters by hand and sent them by mail. Social media did not exist like it does today.

One day I was on my porch and I noticed a commotion among a group of children at the housing project. They were surrounding a lady with a slender look, fast stride, simple light-colored clothing, blondish gray hair in a bun, closed shoes, and a black purse from which you could see tracts, her Bible, and papers overflowing. It appeared that she asked the children for an address that she had penciled on a piece of paper. Attracted by her curious accent when she spoke Spanish, the children guided her to the location. She looked toward where I stood, saw the apartment number, thanked the children for their help, and without saying a thing, went up the stairwell and knocked at my door. I opened it, and to my surprise she said to me, "¿Nereida?" I said yes, with a surprised look and a bit of disbelief. She walked in and appeared agitated. She asked me if she could sit and I assented. She took out a handkerchief from her purse and dried the sweat from her forehead. I offered her a glass of water, which she accepted and drank. I continued to be amazed at her presence, but there she was. She greeted my parents, who decided to leave me alone with her in the living room. She started to explain the reason for her presence in my house. She told me she was a missionary of the Mennonite churches of Puerto Rico. That I had written to the program and they had given her my address because she was starting a new church in Ponce. She told me of the persons who made up the small group in Villa del Carmen. Then, she asked me to get my Bible and, without hardly letting me talk, started to read texts, which she asked me to mark. She gave me some tracts and invited me to her meetings. That's how she ended up staying for two hours.

When she decided to leave, I asked if she would allow me to accompany her to the place where she had left her car, a small light green Toyota Corolla. I explained to her that her feat of walking between blocks in a place where strangers are not welcome was a bit daring. The children followed us, asking her questions about her accent, since she spoke Spanish with difficulty, although I understood her very well. Her fast way of walking, her pale-colored clothing, her hair in a bun, and her way of talking Spanish grabbed everyone's attention, and they asked me "Who is she, and why did she come this way?"

From that day on, it was common to see her arrive at my house, and she became my teacher. She sought me and took me to meetings, where I got to know very friendly people whom I learned to appreciate. I went with her to several Mennonite churches in the center of the island.

Sometimes she irritated me a bit, because something that Gladys Widmer had was perseverance. I learned from her to set aside my insecurities and timidness. She helped me to improve my

166

singing and leadership abilities. She was special to me during family crises.

I created many anecdotal memories with her, but there is a charming one that I recall well because I laughed so much. She came to pick me up. I think my friend Raquel was with me that day in the car when we were traveling with Gladys to a new church in Guayanilla. On our way a police officer stopped her. She got somewhat nervous because she couldn't understand why she was stopped, since she was not driving at an excessive speed. That's what she told the police officer who responded to her. "That's precisely why I stopped you, because you are going at a speed under the minimum speed limit for this highway and that can cause an accident." With her habitual way of talking, she apologized and she told the police officer she would try to drive at the minimum speed limit. This meant that Raquel and I had to take charge the rest of the way by reminding Gladys to speed-up each time she went below the minimum speed limit.

She would always ask Raquel to prepare rice with sausage because she liked the way Raquel prepared it. Sometimes she prepared delicious meals from her place of origin and invited us to share at the table. I didn't like it when she made coffee because she made it too weak, and I am a lover of dark, strong coffee. But I did enjoy her desserts; they were delicious.

Audacious, tireless, persevering, conservative and very dynamic, that's how I remember her.

Although we were not always in agreement, I think of her in my memories. In my heart Gladys Widmer has a special place. I will remember her always as a great woman of God who dedicated herself with a lot of passion.

Nereida Rodríguez Mattei

Gladys Widmer opened her house to me when I was beginning my nursing studies at La Universidad Católica de Puerto Rico in the city of Ponce. I lived with her for about six months. I considered her a mother, teacher, friend and housemate, all in one person. She loved the way I cooked rice for her. When she was hungry for rice, she would say: *"tengo hambre por arroz."* I was tickled by how she spoke Spanish. For example, when I traveled with her in her car, she would say: *"Esta carretera tiene muchas hoyas."* I loved Gladys, and I remember her with fondness and appreciation.

Raquel Trinidad

Gladys Catherine Widmer was born on December 7, 1915, to Daniel W. Widmer and Mary Schlatter Graber in the community of Noble, Washington County, Iowa. She had two brothers, Dale and Maynard.

She graduated from Wayland High School in 1934 and Goshen College in 1942, with degrees in Bible and education. Later she attended New York Theological Seminary, Associated Mennonite Biblical Seminaries, University of Iowa, and New York University.

Gladys taught elementary school from 1942 to 1945 in Wayland, Iowa. She served as secretary for J.D. Graber when he was appointed as the first General Secretary of the Mennonite Board of Missions in Elkhart, Indiana. J.D. was also from Noble, Iowa and was Gladys's uncle. She went on to serve as J.D.'s assistant for five years, from 1945 to 1950, which trained her well for a lifetime in missions.

From 1951 to 1981, Gladys served as a missionary in Puerto Rico; New York City; the Quad Cities; Muscatine, Iowa; and Goshen, Indiana. Each of these settings had large Spanish-speaking populations.

Beth E. Graybill, a researcher who specializes in Mennonite and Amish women, wrote an article[1] in which she made several observations about Gladys's career as a missionary. She noted that Gladys was originally assigned to teach at Betania Mennonite School in Puerto Rico. Gladys and mission personnel soon realized that teaching was not a good fit for her, but she was good at winning new converts. So she was re-assigned to serve as a full-time evangelist and church planter. Gladys planted churches in Bayamón, Coamo, and Ponce, Puerto Rico, and later in Brooklyn, New York, and the Quad Cities and Muscatine, Iowa.

Graybill also observed in her article that Gladys never led revival meetings or baptized. She relied on missionary pastors to come in and do formal preaching. She also discovered or developed local male leaders, taking on public leadership only when she felt she had to do it for lack of anyone else being available. Graybill noted that other leaders recognized that Gladys was a *de facto* church leader. In fact, at its annual assembly in 1982, the Convención de Iglesias Evangélicas Menonitas de Puerto Rico recorded that Gladys "served in a pastoral function and had helped start churches, though she had never been ordained."

In her article, Graybill also quotes Gladys reflecting on her missionary life as follows:

> Finding my place as a lady missionary was not always easy. Many mistakes were made in the learning process .... I am discovering more how to rely on the Holy Spirit to know when to step in, and when to stand back in giving advice, guidance, encouragement, moral support.

In her final retirement years in Goshen, she was a member of College Mennonite Church and attended Iglesia Menonita del Buen Pastor. She died on December 3, 2006, at the age of 90.

Rolando Santiago

25

WANDA BRUNK ZIMMERLY

Wanda was born on January 3, 1936 in Lima, Ohio. In 1956 she began nurse's training at the Lima Memorial Hospital. In 1963 she volunteered in VS and was sent to Puerto Rico. After six weeks of language school she went to work in the operating room, delivery room, and the central sterilization room. During her time off she was involved in VS and church activities. She attended Aibonito Mennonite Church. After two years she became the Director of Nursing at the Mennonite Hospital. In 1974 she began working with Dr. Ronald Graber, assisting him in the operating room, in the office and being on call with him. She married Dr. John

Zimmerly in Dec. 2000, and returned to the States. They now live in The Apostolic Christian Retirement Village near Rittman, Ohio.

———◦◦———

W anda Brunk's service in Puerto Rico had a significant impact on me. She is my mother's first cousin, so I've known her all my life. Growing up in rural Ohio, Wanda was the first person to introduce me to a culture different from my own. Once, when she visited our home, I was excited to watch her prepare a meal for us with Puerto Rican foods. As a child, I was especially fascinated by the *pasteles* wrapped in banana leaves and boiling in the pot! One year she brought me a very special gift— a musical instrument made out of a gourd, a *guiro*. Later, what a memorable experience to fly with my parents to visit Wanda in Puerto Rico!

My interest in the Spanish language began when Wanda's parents returned from visiting her with a coloring book for me with words in Spanish. I studied Spanish in high school and college and very much wanted to serve in a Spanish-speaking country. After graduating from college, my wife and I taught in Bolivia with Mennonite Central Committee.

Wanda lived a life of hospitality. In addition to warmly welcoming many visitors from the U.S. mainland over the years, she helped to make possible the very significant trip to Puerto Rico with my wife and children, along with my in-laws, Justus and Salome Holsinger. She invited all of us to stay in her home, while she stayed at a friend's home.

I credit much of my interest in learning Spanish and serving abroad to the influence of Wanda Brunk Zimmerly and her life of Christian service.

Keaton Shenk

 anda Brunk arrived in Puerto Rico in 1963 to work as a

nurse. She and I were housemates. We lived in Aibonito near the hospital. I had come in 1960. We both attended the Mennonite Church in Aibonito, which was close to our house. Wanda spent some time with the *Diaconado* and helped the church in that way.

She also helped a family with three girls. Wanda would go to their house to help the mother get the girls ready for church. The father had disabilities due to arthritis. The youngest was a young baby when Wanda started to help the family. Gloria, the youngest, would call Wanda "Mami Wanda."

When Gloria was old enough to go to school, Wanda was the one who helped her get ready for school.

Wanda made many carrot cakes. Gloria helped Wanda sell the cakes and the proceeds helped Gloria go to school.

Wanda was the one who drove the car. She would pick up persons to go to church or into town.

Wanda helped many people who needed to have dressings changed after surgery. She was the director of nursing and later worked with Dr. Ron Graber in his office and also helped him in the operating room.

Wanda and I traveled together to Mennonite World Conference when the conference was in Brazil. We also went to Switzerland and Africa. In Switzerland we visited a family we had gotten to know in Puerto Rico. The father was a doctor who had come to Puerto Rico for part of his training to be a surgeon and had worked for a time with Dr. Graber. Their first baby was born in Puerto Rico. We had a good time visiting them.

Wanda got married December 2000 and then went to the States to live.

Mim Godshall

W anda Brunk Zimmerly is one of those beautiful souls who invested her life and energy in the Mennonite work on the Island. I first met her in the early 1960s when she was living with several other nurses in an old wood-frame house on the outskirts of Aibonito, on the way towards Coamo. From the beginning

Wanda connected with me in a very special way and always treated me with appreciation and respect. It is a gift to our Mennonite Puerto Rican community that this friend from Ohio continued to live and work on our Island for a number of decades, offering her services first at the Mennonite hospital and later in Dr. Ronald Graber's office.

Wanda was genuinely humble and kind, completely devoted to a life of service. I will always remember her attention and love towards the elderly. A good example of this was her practice for a period of time of providing transportation for Doña Ramona, an elderly woman in her 90s, to Sunday morning services in our congregation. She would then care for Doña Ramona throughout the afternoon until the evening church activities. One weekend Wanda asked me if my wife Christine and I could substitute for her, picking up Doña Ramona on Sunday morning, providing meals for her during the day, caring for the dear lady throughout the afternoon, and then taking her to church for the evening service. This opportunity, which at first intimidated me, enriched my experience and helped move me toward more compassion and understanding of the elderly. Thank you very much, Wanda.

Her kindness was also evident with our youth group. Wanda would participate in our activities and would also make our birthdays a special occasion. Especially unforgettable to me was the party she planned in her home in September, 1971, for three or four of us who had birthdays that month. Many of our youth group members came to celebrate with us, all clustered into the limited living room space of the Villa Rosales home she shared with Mim Godshall. It was on that occasion, as I moved around the room greeting guests, that I first met Christine Yoder, who was participating in Mennonite Voluntary Service on the Island and teaching Advanced English at Academia Menonita Betania. That initial connection gradually led to a deeper friendship and subsequently to marriage in December, 1972. We have now been married for almost 50 years. Thank you, Wanda, for creating this opportunity that has unquestionably changed my life.

Although we left Puerto Rico in 1976, my contacts with

Wanda have continued. On my sabbatical year to the Island in 1989-90, we would encounter Wanda in church and would chat for a while, catching up on each other's life. She also invited us on a couple of special outings, such as eating fish in Salinas and enjoying the Isla Verde beach. Our two sons, Christine, and I always enjoyed her pleasant and thoughtful companionship.

Wanda Brunk Zimmerly, now married, lives in Ohio, and with her husband visits us periodically on their trips to Indiana. We have also had the pleasure of seeing her in occasional Mennonite/Puerto Rican gatherings, and we always give each other a heartfelt *abrazo puertorriqueño*. For me, Wanda is a special soul who has blessed the Mennonite work on the Island and for whom we can be enormously grateful!

Rafael Falcón

EPILOGUE

Maya Angelou, an African American poet, once wrote that "a hero is any person really intent on making this a better place for all people." This book is a story of many people committed to making a difference, to making this a better world for all of us. Each story in the book is a unique thread that comes together to create a beautiful tapestry of colors and diversity for all of us to enjoy and to remember.

The story of the Mennonites in Puerto Rico is a story that brought together persons from Hesston, Sugar Grove, Coamo Arriba, Chicago, Cidra, Fisher, Harleysville, Aibonito, India, Argentina, and Canada, to name a few of the places of origin. In God's infinite wisdom, a community was built, institutions were born, lives were changed, and a chapter in God's story began. It is evident that this was not easy, and many difficult decisions were made. Families, friends, and loved ones were left behind by those who responded to God's call to move to a strange land with a different language and culture.

As you read each of the stories, you will see that this has also been a story of love. First of all love towards God, that led each of the persons written about to follow a call that they felt God had laid upon them. They said "Yes" when God asked them to follow a path of service and love. It is a story of learning to love each other and becoming one people, regardless of their background and where they came from. It was a profound love that led to the creation of hospitals, schools, churches, and many other ways in which the community could be served and experience the love of God. God's love was expressed in the maternity ward, where thousands of babies were born with the assistance of a number of these workers and out in the field as others were taught the science of poultry farming and flower growing. It was a love that was expressed in the classrooms, whether in the math class or science class, actively talking about faith and its intersection with daily living. It was a love that extended to the living rooms and homes of so many that were willing to open their doors.

This is a story of the commitment of persons who dedicated their lives to expressing the Gospel in many different ways, all helping to make this a better world. They had a commitment not only to serve but to become part of the community in which they lived. It is a story about commitment in helping to develop leaders, as some of those they were serving became their partners in the ministry, and their friends. It is a story about the willingness to leave behind their extended family to become part of a new family bound together by God's love and the understanding that we are all God's children.

The stories of each of these persons are stories of servant leadership. They are stories about persons who became part of the local setting, establishing friendships and building trust with those they were called to serve and live among. There are many such stories, and these pages only reflect a few: stories of unselfishness, of placing others before themselves and genuinely caring for others' needs before worrying about their own. This included calling others to service and leadership and having a willingness to at times move aside as the student became the teacher!

These are stories about how a small group of people planted the seeds that are still contributing to making this a better world. We cannot talk about the poultry industry in Puerto Rico today without going back to some of the stories that are found in this book. We could also look at education and the role that the Academia Menonita in Summit Hills and Academia Menonita

Betania has played in the education and leadership of many; including a number of those educated who in later years heard God's call to cross the pond to the north and help build God's Kingdom among those who at one point were the ones sending people to serve.

To some extent, this is the story of the Sistema de Salud Menonita, which today counts six hospitals, six urgent care centers (including one in the Puerto Rican island of Culebra), medical insurance, and hospice and home health services. Interwoven into the threads of many of the persons that we have read about is the story of the birth of medical services to serve society. When the hospital started in the *barrio* La Plata, it would have been hard to visualize what the impact was going to be years later. The seeds of love have grown beyond what could have been imagined.

In some ways, these are stories of beginnings, of institutions that were born out of a commitment to spread God's love by responding to society's needs evident at that particular time. It is also a story of beginnings, of churches that were built and congregations that were established. But the stories in the book go beyond institutions, congregations, or buildings. It is a human story of hearts that were touched and changed, creating a path forward in which so many people have been impacted. This is a story about deep friendships that were created, that extended far beyond the years of formal service. This is a story of families that were born and created by love and compassion to others. This is the story of new families that were brought together, some born in the continental United States and others born in "*el campo puertoriqueño*" and became brothers and sisters and carried the same name. It is about long-term friendships that were born and are still strong many years later, not just among the first ones but with the families that followed; and just as we read in the book of Ruth, "thy people shall be my people."

The title of this book, *They Made a Difference,* is so appropriate. In every storyline in the book, you can see and feel how the persons mentioned made a difference to make this a better world.

They are stories of love, commitment, servant leadership, and about planting seeds that are still producing and making an impact in Puerto Rican society and beyond. There are still many untold stories, and in the book you may get a glimpse of some of them.

But perhaps as you finish reading the book, you will realize that the story is not finished, that chapters are still being written, lives are still being touched, and the impact from those beginnings has grown far beyond the bounds of the island of Puerto Rico, to North America and beyond! The story is just beginning, and just as the scripture tells us in Revelation 3:8, God has an "open door that no one can shut." Let's see what awaits us in the future as God's story continues to be written.

Carlos Romero

OTHERS WHO SERVED

MOSES BEACHY

> Moses erved in the La Plata project and later as a pastor in Guavate.

JOHN BRANDEBERRY

> John was instrumental in the beginnings of the poultry industry in Puerto Rico.

LUKE BIRKY

Luke was the business manager of the La Plata project and later helped raise funds for the Aibonito hospital.

RICHARD BURKHOLDER

Richard worked at Escuela Menonita Betania teaching shop, later principal of the Academia Menonita Summit Hills.

ROBERT EHRET

Robert was a funeral director. He contributed space in his facilities for the San Juan church to meet.

JORGE GONZÁLEZ

Jorge was active in Conservative Mennonite churches in U.S. for many years.

RONALD GRABER

Ronald was a surgeon at the Aibonito Mennonite Hospital for 32 years, from 1965 to 1997.

DON HEISER

Don was a pastor of the Aibonito Mennonite Church and others.

R.J AND FLORENCE HOWER

R.J. and Florence were nurses in the Aibonito hospital for decades; they adopted two Puerto Rican children.

MARTHA KANAGY

Martha taught science and music at Betania for a number of years.

SIMON LIECHTY

Simon was involved in mission work in Puerto Rico for twenty years, in the areas of agriculture and construction. Simon and his wife Leah adopted three Puerto Rican children.

CARLOS AND MABEL LUGO

Carlos and Mabel taught at Escuela Menonita Betania for many years.

MARJORIE SHANTZ MARTIN

Marjorie was born in Cambridge, Ontario, Canada. She served as a nurse-midwife in Puerto Rico from 1947 to 1970. Part of her legacy is the story that at times she would deliver three babies in three different homes all within 24 hours.

MERCEDES MELÉNDEZ

Mercedes taught second grade in the Academia Menonita Betania for many years. She was also very active in the life of the Mennonite church in Puerto Rico.

MERVIN NAFZIGER

Mervin was hospital administrator in Aibonito for seven years.

DAVID POWELL

David was pastor of several Mennonite churches and director of the Instituto Bíblico Menonita.

ESTEBAN RIVERA

Esteban, from La Plata, was one of the first Puerto Rican Mennonites. He and his wife Neida worked at the Aibonito General

Hospital for many years.

EILEEN ROLÓN

Eileen was active in church work and served for years at the Aibonito Mennonite Hospital.

SAMUEL ROLÓN

Samuel served as pastor at several Mennonite churches in Puerto Rico. From 1968-1970, he and his family served as missionaries to Spanish-speakers in Brussels, Belgium. He also worked as a social worker in Puerto Rico and in Reading and Lancaster, Pennsylvania, where he primarily served the Latino community. He died in 2018.

JOSÉ A. SANTIAGO

José was a pastor and worked with Librería Cristiana Unida, a Mennonite bookstore in Puerto Rico. In Lancaster, Pennsylvania, he was responsible for planting Spanish-speaking churches. Also, he was the first Mennonite missionary in Venezuela.

MELQUIADES SANTIAGO

Melquiades was a well-known Mennonite pastor from La Plata. He was also a prosperous businessman.

VIRGINIA SHOWALTER

Virginia worked as a nurse at the Hospital General Menonita for many years. She was also very active in the life of the church.

ELVIN V. SNYDER

Elvin V. Snyder was born near Breslau, Ontario, Canada in 1900. Snyder studied at Goshen College, Goshen, Indiana, earning a B.A. in 1927. In 1928 he married Mary Fretz. He was a missionary for many years with the Mennonite Board of Missions. He served in Argentina, Puerto Rico and South Texas. He taught at Eastern Mennonite College from 1970 to 1973, and was later pastor of the Spanish Mennonite Church in Milwaukee, Wisconsin.

In Puerto Rico, Snyder served from 1953 to 1965 in a variety of church and educational positions He died in Elkhart, Indiana in 1985.

ROYAL SNYDER

Royal was involved in agriculture, including the beginnings of the Puerto Rico poultry industry. He also taught shop at Academia Menonita Betania. The Snyders adopted three Puerto Rican children.

MERLE SOMMERS

Merle taught music at the Escuela Menonita Betania and later was principal for several years.

ELMER SPRINGER

Elmer worked at the Ulrich Foundation for many years.

GERALD WILSON

Gerald was principal at Escuela Menonita Betania for seven years.

MARY ELLEN YODER

Mary Ellen worked in Audición Luz y Verdad for many years. She was also very active in the life of the Mennonite church on the Island, especially in the Coamo congregation.

SOME WHO SERVED IN CHURCH LEADERSHIP POSITIONS

(Information from the *Mennonite Yearbook and Directory*, 1956-1972)

RAMÓN BARRETO
Pastor at Guavate, 1971-1972.

JUAN BERDECÍA
Pastor at Usabón, 1959-1960.

EUGENE CARPER
Principal at Academia Menonita de Summit Hills, 1972.

JOSÉ DELGADO
Pastor at Usabón, 1962-1967.

AMBROSIO ENCARNACIÓN
Pastor at Palo Hincado, 1967-1970; Vice-president, Puerto Rico Mennonite Conference, 1971; pastor at Aibonito, 1971-1972.

DAVID GROH
Administrator, Aibonito Mennonite Hospital, 1958.

JAMES HAMILTON
Administrator, Aibonito Mennonite Hospital, 1972.

RAY LANDIS
Pastor at Smirna, 1962-1964; pastor at Bayamón, 1968.

JOHN LEHMAN
President, Instituto Bíblico Menonita, 1961; Principal at Escuela Menonita Betania, 1961.

ELOY LEÓN
Treasurer, Puerto Rico Mennonite Conference, 1962-1963.

JORGE MELÉNDEZ
Pastor at Cidra, 1969-1970.

HERBERT NEFF
Administrator, La Plata Mennonite Hospital, 1957.

WILFREDO ROIG
Pastor at Asomante, 1966-1967.

RAÚL ROSADO
Pastor at La Plata, 1966-1972.

SERGIO ROSARIO
President, Puerto Rico Mennonite Conference, 1970; pastor at Cayey, 1970; pastor at Coamo, 1972.

JOSÉ M. ROSARIO
Pastor at Botijas, 1969; pastor at Cayey, 1970; President, Puerto Rico Mennonite Conference 1970; pastor at Palo Hincado, 1971-1972.

J.W. SHANK
Pastor at La Plata, 1956.

RUTH THOMAS
Principal at Academia Menonita de Summit Hills, 1964-1967.

VICENTE VALES
Pastor at Asomante and Betania, 1971-1972; Treasurer Puerto Rico Mennonite Conference, 1971-1972.

HÉCTOR VARGAS
Pastor at Asomante, 1965; pastor at Bayamón, 1969-1972.

ABOUT THE CONTRIBUTORS

GRACE ULRICH BECKER

Grace Ulrich Becker, daughter of Raymond and Verda Ulrich, was secretary for the Ulrich Foundation for many years. Grace and her husband, Paul, live in Bismarck, Illinois.

LUKE BIRKY

Luke served in Puerto Rico at the La Plata Project from 1947 to 1953 in maintenance, purchasing, and as business manager. On returning to the States he spent six months fund-raising for the new hospital in Aibonito. Beginning in 1954, he served in a variety of administrative roles in hospitals in Rocky Ford and La Junta, ultimately as the administrator of the La Junta Mennonite Hospital and Sanitarium from 1958-1966. From 1966 to 1979 he served as Secretary for Health and Welfare of the Mennonite Board of Missions and Charities in Elkhart, Indiana. From 1979 to 1987 he was administrator of the Mennonite Retirement Home in Albany, Oregon. He and his wife, Verna, were co-leaders of the Goshen College Study-Service Term program in Costa Rica from 1987 to 1988. Luke lives at Greencroft Communities in Goshen, Indiana.

CONSUELO ORTIZ BRENNER

Consuelo graduated from Escuela Menonita Betania in 1963. After high school, she moved to Philadelphia and served in a voluntary service unit. In 1969 she married Albert Brenner from Spartansburg, Pennsylvania, where they have a dairy farm, sell farm equipment, and raise crops. They have three married daughters and seven grandchildren. Currently Albert and Consuelo spend the winter months in Sarasota, Florida.

LILLIAM COLÓN

Lilliam was born to Juan Colón and María Celina Ortiz in Puerto Rico, where she grew up. She studied in Academia Menonita Betania and in the public school. She graduated from the University of Puerto Rico and worked as a teacher. She is married to Alwin González and has two daughters and two grandchildren. She is retired and lives in Cape Coral, Florida.

BRUCE GLICK

Bruce has worked for Goshen College and spent four years in Bolivia working for Mennonite Central Committee. He now lives in Goshen, Indiana.

MIRIAM GODSHALL

Mim Godshall studied nursing in a program at the local hospital. After graduating, she worked at the hospital for two years in pediatrics. She then decided to go into VS and went to Puerto Rico in September, 1960, as a nurse at the Hospital Menonita. In 1975, the Department of Health offered a course in midwifery with the Hospital Universitario in San Juan, and she was asked to take the course so she could take care of the prenatal clinic and women in labor. After taking the course and graduating she began delivering babies, delivering over 4,600 during her time in Puerto Rico. She now lives in Harrisonburg, Virginia.

Stan Godshall

Stan and his wife, Susan, served in I-W service at Hospital Menonita in Aibonito in 1971 -`1973. They served with Stan's older sister, Miriam Godshall, who worked as an obstetrical nurse at the hospital most of the 57 years that she lived and served there. Stan enjoyed his ham radio hobby along with Dr Ronald Graber during his years at Aibonito. Stan and Susan returned to Lancaster County in 1973, where Stan joined new a group family practice called Norlanco Famly Health Center in Elizabethtown. He practiced there for 40 years with a several 1-2 year stints of service (5 years total) at Shirati Hospital in Tanzania, East Africa. Stan and Susan now have three adult children and 10 grandchildren. Stan retired from his medical practice in 2013 and a few years later they moved to Harrisonburg, Virginia, to be closer to their family.

Rachel Greaser Good

Rachel Greaser Good was born to Lawrence and Annabelle Greaser in La Plata, Puerto Rico, joining her four older brothers. She grew up in Aibonito, Puerto Rico, attending Escuela Menonita Betania through the 9th grade. Rachel and her parents transitioned to Goshen, Indiana, in 1971. Rachel and her husband, Stephen Good, have three grown children and seven grandchildren. They are members of Harvest Community Church in Goshen, Indiana.

Rachel worked in the Latin America office at Mennonite Board of Missions in Elkhart, Indiana, for nine years and experienced the sending aspect of missions. In 2005 she and Steve moved to Mozambique, where they did development work with World Relief for 12 years. They are currently serving with Zambia Works in Mongu, Zambia, and have grown to love Africa while also missing the Latin American culture.

GALEN D. GREASER

Galen grew up in Puerto Rico as part of the Lawrence and Annabelle (Troyer) Greaser household. He attended Betania and Aibonito High School, graduating from Inter-American University in San Germán in 1969. Galen obtained an M.A. degree in Latin American Studies at the University of Texas at Austin and worked as a freelance translator for several years. He was then employed as the translator and curator of the Spanish Collection of the Texas General Land Office for twenty-eight years before retiring in 2011. Galen lives in Austin, Texas, with his wife Carmen Ramos.

ROBIN HELMUTH

Robin arrived in Puerto Rico in 1961 at age 4 with his parents and two younger brothers. Within four years, two more brothers were added. Even today he has no trouble picturing the many homes the family rented, the many churches it attended or visited, and the many friends, neighbors and classmates he had. He can also picture the coffee plants and flamboyans and taste the fresh *guayabas*, *fresas*, *quenepas*, *tamarindos*, *mangós*, and many more. But, the aroma of freshly baked pan *de manteca* is indelibly etched in his brain.

In 1996 he took his wife and two young children back to the island, along with his parents. The children were able to experience a little bit of what he did from 1961 thru 1973, even catching lizards, trying to find the elusive *coquíes* and knocking down *cocos* to crack open for a snack. To this day, his children state the Puerto Rico visit was their favorite trip ever! He agrees.

After more than 30 years working as a pathologist and laboratory medical director in the Indianapolis area, he is mostly retired. He strive to continue learning something each day, having a little fun each day and doing something nice for someone each day. He has no doubt these goals were formulated many years ago while he was being blessed to be an honorary *borinqueño*.

ELENA ORTIZ HERSHBERGER

Elena taught second grade at Escuela Menonita Betania from 1966—68. In the States, she taught Spanish and cross-cultural studies at Mount Union and Malone Universities in Ohio. Elena has done translating and tutoring, writes poetry, and recently published a children's book. She is now retired and lives in Canton, Ohio, with her husband Lowell Hershberger.

GENE HERSHEY

Born in Chicago, Illinois, Gene first went to Puerto Rico with his parents and two older sisters at the age of four months. At 17, he returned to the U.S. where he attended Hesston College, then graduated from Easter Mennonite University in 1969. He spent the next two years in the jungles of Peru, working with Wycliffe Bible Translators. Returning to the U.S., he earned his FAA commercial and maintenance licenses at Moody Bible Institute's missionary aviation flight school. After studying linguistics at the University of Oklahoma, he returned to Peru as a missionary pilot with JAARS, Wycliffe's technical division. He later transferred to Bolivia, after which he returned to the U.S. where he flew as a corporate pilot. He also worked as a commercial pilot based in Singapore and Beijing. He retired as a corporate pilot in 2013, and now lives outside of Richmond, Virginia, on an airpark, where he remains active flying his experimental airplane and serves in a local church. He has two daughters, a stepdaughter and three grandchildren.

DAVID HOLSINGER

Dave Holsinger lived in Puerto Rico for almost four of his pre-school years. His parents, Justus and Salome Holsinger, gave two terms of service in La Plata. The family returned to the States in 1952 and settled in Hesston, Kansas. Dave attended schools in Kansas, graduating from Kansas State with a degree in Mechanical Engineering. He was employed in the petroleum industry for nearly 40 years. Dave and his wife Jan are now retired and living in Houston, Texas. They enjoy worldwide travel and family time with their three sons in Texas and with their eight year old grandson Justus.

LUIS ELIER RODRÍGUEZ

Luis Elier Rodríguez was born in Ponce, Puerto Rico. His three sons are Luis Elier, Irvin and Rubiel Rodríguez. Luis Elier has a Master of Divinity (MDiv) degree from the Evangelical Seminary of Puerto Rico. He made his residency in clinical pastoral education at Presbyterian Hospital in Albuquerque, New Mexico. From there he went to the Baptist Health System in San Antonio, Texas, where he did a specialty toward becoming a certified educator of the Association of Clinical Pastoral Education of the U.S. He has a doctorate in ministry (DMin) from McCormick Theological Seminary in Chicago. Currently he is in charge of the program in Clinical Pastoral Education at Houston Methodist Hospital in Houston, Texas.

ÁNGEL LUIS MIRANDA

Ángel Luis taught at the Escuela Menonita Betania and with the Public Department of Education. He also worked as pastor of Summit Hills, as Mennonite Voluntary Service coordinator, and as guidance counselor for the Summit

Hills Academy. He was instrumental in the founding of the Bayamón church and served as chaplain for the Hospice Program at the Aibonito Mennonite Hospital. Ángel Luis also served as chaplain in the Cayey Mennonite Hospital. In the States he was pastor at the Alice Mennonite Church and conference administrator in Texas. He now resides in Greencroft Communities, Goshen, Indiana, with his wife, Lora Esch.

ERIC MIRANDA

Born in Aibonito at Hospital Menonita, Eric Miranda is the youngest of Ángel Luis and Lora Miranda's three children. But calling him young at this point is a stretch! In 1981, the Miranda family moved from Puerto Rico to Elkhart, Indiana, so his father could pursue graduate seminary studies at AMBS. Eric, 14 at the time, attended Bethany Christian High School and, later, Goshen College, spending his junior year studying French in Strasbourg, France. After Goshen, he worked as a flight attendant for American Airlines, at first based in New York, and then Chicago, where he has lived ever since. At the eleven-year mark of being a flight attendant, he took advantage of an early retirement offer in order to be a full-time singer. Presently, Eric performs with the Chicago Symphony Chorus, the Grant Park Chorus, Bella Voce, and Newberry Consort. His professional patchwork also includes teaching private voice lessons, medical interpreting for Spanish-speaking patients, and translation. Eric and his spouse, Charles Thomas, live in Rogers Park, Chicago's most diverse neighborhood. As such, neighborhood grocery stores stock all manner of cooking ingredients, which Charles and Eric can access to try recipes from all over the world, including Puerto Rico, of course. Eric and Charles also enjoy traveling, particularly to places where friends live, and, in the winter, to warm climates like Puerto Rico's.

MARY MIRANDA

Mary Miranda served as an elementary school teacher for 11 years, then worked another 11 as Human Resources Director of the Mennonite Hospital of Aibonito, becoming one of the founding members of the Society of Human Resource Managers of Health Agencies in Puerto Rico. Later she was the Human Resources Manager for Westinghouse and Cutler Hammer (Eaton). She has been a facilitator for both Dale Carnegie and Steven Covey courses and a consultant in the areas of labor relations and personal development.

She is the author of the books *Un hijo de Mallorca en Puerto Rico*; *Manual para la Búsqueda, Retención y el Éxito en el Empleo*; *Memorias del Cerro de Pulguillas, la historia contada por su gente*; *Historia de la Avicultura en Puerto Rico, la contribución de Stanley Miller y otros avicultores*; *Despierta: Todo está en ti*; and *Nuestro Camino Interior*, the last two widely distributed in Puerto Rico and Latin America. Her writings have been published in various newspapers and magazines of the Island.

She is a community leader and founder of the SiembrAmor organization and is president of the Junta Directiva del Centro de Ayuda Social PASO in Aibonito, which provides services to people in need.

LINDA ULRICH NUSSBAUM

Linda Ulrich Nussbaum and her husband, Harry, returned to Aibonito in 2009, 33 years after Linda's father, Raymond Ulrich, completed the mission work of the Ulrich Foundation. Linda and Harry felt the call of God to restore the old historic Serrallés house, which Raymond Ulrich bought during Ulrich Foundation days; using the house again to serve the community of Aibonito. With permission from the current owner, Carlos Rivera, teams came to help Linda and Harry restore the house. In 2013 the house took on the name "Casa Ulrich" and was opened to the public.

Visitors came to tour through the house and learn of its history, spend time in the prayer room, shop in the resale shop, relax with friends in the cafe or stay for a night. The house was also open for events. After Hurricane María in 2017, the house was closed to the public. Linda and Harry began hosting work teams coming through Mennonite Disaster Service to help repair roofs on houses that were damaged by the hurricane. In 2019, the house was put back into the hands of the Rivera family to continue serving the community of Aibonito. Linda and Harry are now retired and living near Chattanooga, Tennessee.

Enrique Ortiz

Enrique worked as a mechanic at Ulrich Foundation and served in I-W at the Casa de Salud in Aibonito. Later, he worked in maintenance in government housing and at the Academia Menonita Betania. He served as pastor in the Aibonito and Summit Hills Mennonite churches and as Executive Secretary of the Convención de Iglesias Evangélicas Menonitas de Puerto Rico. Since 2011 Enrique has lived in Greencroft Communities, Goshen, Indiana.

José M. Ortiz

José was a teacher in Escuela Menonita Betania and in Academia Menonita Summit Hills. He served as pastor in the Palo Hincado, La Cuchilla, and Summit Hills Mennonite churches in Puerto Rico, as well as in churches in Goshen, Indiana, and New Holland, Pennsylvania. After moving to the States he served in the Office of Latin Concerns with the General Board of the Mennonite Church. He also taught at Goshen College, Goshen, Indiana, and in Eastern Mennonite Seminary, Harrisonburg, Virginia. Before he retired, he worked for Mennonite Central Committee USA from 1999 to 2004. José currently lives in Goshen with his wife, Iraida Rivera.

NEREIDA RODRÍGUEZ MATTEI

Nereida Rodríguez Mattei was born and raised in Ponce, Puerto Rico. She studied in public schools and attended the Pontifical Catholic University of Puerto Rico, where she obtained a B.A. in elementary education and special education, and a Master's degree in education (MEd), with a concentration in curriculum and instruction. She worked more than 30 years as a licensed special education teacher in the public school system. She is currently retired, living in the city of Clermont, Florida, where she dedicates time to her family, especially her granddaughters. She always enjoys singing, reading, and writing.

CARLOS ROMERO

Carlos Romero was born into a Catholic family in Puerto Rico. He attended Academia Menonita in Summit Hills, Puerto Rico, and earned a bachelor's degree in international relations from Bradley University and a master's in church management from the Graduate Theological Foundation.

From 1985 to 1990, Romero served as the administrator for Academia Menonita. While in Puerto Rico he served on the executive committee of the Puerto Rico Mennonite Conference. From 1990 to 1999, Romero worked for the Mennonite Board of Congregational Ministries as the denominational minister of youth and youth convention coordinator. From 1999 to 2002, he served as vice president of student life and dean of students at Goshen College.

Romero and his family served with Mennonite Board of Missions for a short-term assignment in Spain. He was co-founder of Developing Harmony through Diversity in the 1990s, an initiative of the Mennonite Church on dismantling racism.

Romero is presently serving as an administrator in training at Hamilton Grove Retirement Community in New

Carlisle, Indiana.

Romero lives in Goshen, Indiana, with his wife Celina. He has two children, both graduates of Eastern Mennonite University. He is an active member of Waterford Mennonite Church.

ROLANDO SANTIAGO

Rolando served in Puerto Rico as Bible teacher at Academia Menonita Summit Hills from 1981-1984, and edited *Alcance Menonita*, a newsletter of the Convención de Iglesias Evangélicas Menonitas de Puerto Rico. In the United States, he was an evaluator of children's mental health services for the State of New York and for the federal Department of Health and Human Services in Maryland. He served twice with the Mennonite Central Committee U.S., as assistant director from 1979-1981 and as executive director, 2004-2010. Rolando currently is director of Behavioral Health and Crisis Services, Montgomery County, Maryland, and lives with his spouse, Raquel Trinidad, in Silver Spring, Maryland.

BETTY SHENK

She lives with her husband, Keaton, and in Harrisonburg, Virginia. They have three adult sons, Nate, Timothy and David. They and their families live in Goshen, Indiana; Camden, New Jersey; and Harrisonburg, Virginia.

Her parents, Justus and Salome Holsinger, are no longer living, but she feels fortunate to have had many wonderful visits until they passed away at the age of 96 (Justus) and 98 (Salome).

Spending time with her six grandchildren, ages five to 13, is always a highlight! Since retiring as an elementary school counselor several years ago, she values visits with family, traveling, reading, daily walks, and volunteering with her church (Community Mennonite) and organizations such as Gift & Thrift, Bridges Community Gatherings, and Bridge of Hope. Most of these activities have been curtailed due to the pandemic; hopefully some normalcy will return in the coming months.

KEATON SHENK

He has wonderful memories of visits with Wanda Brunk in Puerto Rico and in Ohio, and values his continued contact with Wanda and her husband, John.

Before retiring, he was a teacher of elementary and middle school students in Bolivia (with Mennonite Central Committee), Page County, Virginia, and Harrisonburg, Virginia.

Currently, he's enjoying the freedom and flexibility to explore other ways to be involved in the community and church. With his wife, Betty Holsinger Shenk, he enjoy special times with his parents in Ohio and with their adult children and their families in Indiana, New Jersey, and Virginia.

TED SPRINGER

Ted was born in the Mennonite Hospital at its original site in La Plata. He attended Escuela Menonita Betania through ninth grade and graduated from high school at Robinson School in Santurce, Puerto Rico. He attended Hesston College and Goshen College, where he graduated with a bachelor degree in Biology in 1972. In 1973 he began his career in medical diagnostics research and development at Miles Laboratories, Inc., later Bayer Corporation. The majority of his career involved product development, operations management, international manufacturing and strategic planning at large international medical diagnostics firms. In 2004, Ted joined HandyLab, Inc., a startup company, which successfully developed instruments and diagnostic reagents for the rapid detection of infectious diseases. After the sale of this company, he retired as VP of Manufacturing with BD Diagnostics in Ann Arbor, Michigan. Ted and his wife, Marlene Slagle, enjoy summers in Middlebury, Indiana and winters in Sarasota, Florida and visiting their two adult daughters and grandchildren. He enjoys golf, biking, fishing and the great outdoors, where he is still awed by the wonders of land and sea.

ROGER STUDER

His connection to Puerto Rico started with the VS Unit in Aibonito in 1966. He was honored to work with Lester Hershey and a team consisting of Alta Hershey, Anna K. Massanari, Mary Ellen Yoder, and Jorge Meléndez at Luz y Verdad as a technician responsible for the recording of Spanish language taped messages to be broadcast throughout the world.

Upon leaving Puerto Rico in mid-1968, he went to work in Bloomington, Illinois, as a technician/engineer for various broadcast equipment manufacturers, including Automatic Tape Control, Gates Radio Company/Harris Communications, Sono-Mag Corporation, and International Tapetronics Corporation until 1996, when he started working at the Caterpillar Technical Center, where he stayed until his retirement in 2010. He still lives on the family farm near Roanoke, Illinois, and helps with the grain harvest every year, as well as volunteering at Great Oaks Community Church in various activities including the Garden of Giving, which supplies fresh produce to several food pantries locally. He continues to pursue his lifelong hobby of amateur radio (K9VSK) through participation in The MennoNet each week as well as serving with the Woodford County Repeater Association. He also serves on the board of the Woodford County Historical Genealogy Society. Other hobbies include amateur astronomy and photography as well as road trips with his wife, Karen.

His family consists of his wife, Karen, five children in

Bloomington, Illinois, Elmhurst, Illinois, Edina, Minnesota, and Little Rock, Arkansas, and five grandchildren (soon to be six in May 2021).

ANNABELLE FALCÓN TRIMMER

Annabelle was born and raised in Aibonito, Puerto Rico. She attended Escuela Menonita Betania in Pulguillas, the University of Puerto Rico in Río Piedras and Rutgers University in New Jersey. She worked for Pfizer as a scientist until she retired in 2018.

She lives in Manakin Sabot, Virginia, with her husband Charles and their dogs Lucy and Milo. Annabelle enjoys her retirement and spends her time reading, gardening, walking and shopping.

RAQUEL TRINIDAD

Raquel Trinidad was born in Cayey, Puerto Rico, and raised in barrio Guavate of Cayey, and in The Bronx of New York City. She obtained her BS in nursing at the Pontifical Catholic University of Puerto Rico in Ponce. She started her nursing career at Mennonite General Hospital in Aibonito. Over a 40-year nursing career, she served at Caguas Regional Hospital, Caguas, Puerto Rico; Albany General Hospital, Albany, New York; Shady Grove Adventist Hospital in Gaithersburg, Maryland; and Lancaster General Hospital in Lancaster, Pennsylvania. She is happily retired and is mother to two grown children. She has three grandchildren. She enjoys exercising and caring for her loved ones.

WELDON TROYER

Weldon went to Puerto Rico in 1944 with his parents, Dr. George and Kathryn Troyer. He attended high school at the Baptist Academy of Barranquitas (BAB) from 1946 to 1949, at the time that Stanley Miller was the principal of the school. He returned to the States in 1949, where he attended Hesston College and Goshen College, graduating in 1953. In 1953 he returned to Puerto Rico, where he worked as a laboratory technician at the La Plata Hospital in I-W service. From 1955 to 1959 he attended the University of Puerto Rico School of Medicine. From 1959 to 1960 he was an intern in Indianapolis, then practiced medicine in Goshen, Indiana from 1960 until his retirement in 2002. In 1963 he joined with three other physicians to create the High Park Group, which had the goal of supporting one of the physicians at a time in a year of medical mission service. From 1965-66 he served in Puerto Rico as a physician at the Aibonito Mennonite Hospital. For eight years he was a board member of the Robert D. Ehret Good Samaritan Foundation, a philanthropic organization located in Puerto Rico. Weldon lives in Goshen, Indiana.

RICHARD ULRICH

Richard Ulrich, son of Raymond and Verda Ulrich, served with the Ulrich Foundation from 1965-1975. Richard and his wife, Donna, live in Mineral Wells, Texas.

WANDA BRUNK ZIMMERLY

Wanda was born in Lima, Ohio, to Rudy and Emma (Moore) Brunk. After high school she went to Tanksley, Kentucky, to help in mission work started by her home church. In 1956, she began nurse's training in a three year program at Lima Memorial Hospital, graduating in 1960. After working several years in the Operating Room at Lima Memorial Hospital, she volunteered for Voluntary Service in 1963 and was assigned to the Aibonito Mennonite Hospital. At the end of the two years, she became the Director of Nursing, a position she held for almost nine years. Toward the end of 1974 she started working with Dr. Ronald Graber, assisting him in the operating room, working in the office and being on call with him. When he retired, she returned to the operating room for a short time and then helped in the Nursing Office.

She is married to Dr. John Zimmerly. They are now living in The Apostolic Christian Retirement Village near Rittman, Ohio.

ABOUT THE EDITORS

RAFAEL FALCÓN was born in Aibonito, Puerto Rico. His parents, of Catholic tradition, began attending the La Plata Mennonite Church in 1955 and in that same year registered him as a third-grader in Escuela Menonita Betania. After graduating from Betania as a ninth-grader and completing high school and college, he returned in 1968 to teach junior-high Spanish and Social Studies for two years. From 1973 to 1976 he served as the first Puerto Rican director of the school.

Falcón received his bachelor degree from Inter-American University of Puerto Rico and finished one year of graduate studies at the Universidad de Puerto Rico. He completed his masters and doctoral degrees in Spanish American Literature at the University of Iowa.

He has published books and articles on a variety of themes, including Puerto Rican immigration to the United States, Afro-Hispanic influence in literature, Hispanic culture, and Hispanic Mennonite history. In 1985 Herald Press published his *La Iglesia Menonita Hispana en Norte América: 1932-1982,* as well as its translated version. *Salsa: A Taste of Hispanic Culture* came out in 1998, and in 2008 he published a collection of short stories, *Mi Gente: In Search of the Hispanic Soul.* In addition, he has edited numerous textbooks for the teaching of Spanish as a second language.

Falcón is a retired professor of Spanish language, Spanish American literature, and Hispanic culture from Goshen College, Goshen, Indiana, where he taught for 32 years.

Rafael and his wife, Christine Yoder, are the parents of two adult sons, Bryan Rafael and Brent Daniel, and the proud grandparents of Willow and Sebastian.

TOM LEHMAN was born in eastern Ohio, the son of school teachers who served in mission work for the Mennonite Church in Ethiopia and Puerto Rico.

He completed his undergraduate studies at Goshen College and obtained a graduate degree in Library Science from Indiana University. He retired from the University of Notre Dame Hesburgh Library after working there for 26 years, first as a cataloger and then as Digital Access Librarian.

He edited *My Library Manual* in 2006 and co-edited *Making Library Web Sites Usable* in 2009. In 2013 he published Justus Holsinger's previously unpublished 1970 manuscript *Puerto Rico: Island of Progress.*

For the past eight years he has been digitizing missionary photos taken outside the United States in the mid-20th century. Photos from this collection have been the subject of two books and have appeared in numerous books, magazine articles, and TV shows. They can be seen at www.flickr.com/photos/tlehman/.

Tom is married to Mary Windhorst and has three children, Jason, Kevin, and Jessica. He enjoys paddling and camping in wilderness areas and spending time with his five grandchildren.

34668073R00132